The Genealogist's
GOOGLE TOOLBOX

A Genealogist's Guide to Google

2nd Edition

Lisa Louise Cooke

TABLE OF CONTENTS

INTRODUCTION

I'm in a bit of a predicament as a technology writer. By the time I identify a topic, do my research, write, edit and get ready to flip the switch on publishing, *everything* can change.

And *a lot has changed* since 2011 when I wrote the first edition of *The Genealogist's Google Toolbox*. Many of the genealogy websites and tools that I talked about back then on *The Genealogy Gems Podcast* have come and gone. And even though Google, the giant that it is, is still around, many of the cool tools we talked about in that first edition have disappeared. It's easy to get cranky about such inconvenient changes, but ask yourself: *Do I really want my genealogy research to stagnate?* I know I don't! The advent of the Internet, the growth of databases, the ever evolving web platforms...all of that technological evolution has continually opened new avenues of pursuit in my quest for the answers to my family's past. It's a thrilling time to be a family historian!

So in this edition, I'm not going to spend anytime crying over lost Googly loves. We've got ancestors to find and stories to tell, and this newest edition is chock full of the most up to date information available to assure search success. Not only have I combed through every word and every image, I've dumped the stuff that went bye-bye and devoted new keystrokes to exciting advancements and ideas that will once again kick start your research.

And while I'm incredibly appreciative to those of you who have invested in this new edition after pouring over the last one, I'm keenly aware that lots of new folks will be joining us this time around. That means we need to quickly lay down that same firm foundation of knowledge for them in this introduction. But then we all will fasten our seat belts and jump into the following 21 chapters, several of which are brand spanking new!

Are you ready to Google? ***Let's Go!***

At least as far back as 1907 the advertising slogan of Cleveland, Ohio's American Fork & Hoe Co. "True Temper" tool line was:

THE RIGHT TOOL FOR THE RIGHT JOB.

Company executives knew that it was important to farmers to save time, labor, and money, and their advertising leaflets made a clear case as to how tools made for the job at hand could do just that.

When it comes to your online genealogical research, you also need the top of the line tools to help you get the job done. In this book you will learn how to fill your genealogy toolbox with free state-of-the-art online tools that are built to search, translate, message, and span the globe. In order to get the right tools for the job, we're heading outside the genealogy community, and to the folks who dominate the online world: Google.

Introduction to Google

The big white empty screen of the classic Google webpage < www.google.com > is quite ironic considering the vast amount of free tools offered by Google and the power of their monumental search engine. So while you may have a handle on the basics of search, it's time to take your research to the next level. We will cover a wide range of advanced techniques and tools that will help you get the most from this quiet giant.

Let's Look Under the Hood

In order to really be able to maximize the power of Google search, it's important to understand what goes on behind that search box and big white webpage.

Let's start by refreshing our understanding how Google search works by watching the video *How Search Works* by Google.

VIDEO: How Search Works
http://www.youtube.com/watch?v=BNHR6IQJGZs

Search Strategies for High-Quality Results

It's time to put an end to fruitless Google searches.

What do I mean by fruitless searches? Searches that:
- bring up thousands (if not hundreds of millions!) of results.
- contain websites on topics totally unrelated to your search.
- include websites containing completely unreliable information.

In this chapter we are going to tackle these challenges by looking at why these fruitless searches occur, and how to correct the situation, so we can obtain higher quality results.

Why Fruitless Searches Occur

One of the primary reasons why researchers end up with searches full of countless low-quality results is that they fail to recognize two fundamentals about Google search:

1. Search is an art not an exact science.
2. High quality search results are not the product of single searches, but rather a process.

In other words, there is no one answer for effective searches. Rather, it's critical to understand the tools at your disposal and how to use them in sequence to achieve the desired results.

The primary tools available to the searcher include:
- Basic Search Strategies
- Advanced Search Strategies
- Search Operators
- The Search Options Column

Mixing and matching these tools in a variety of ways (as the particular search scenario requires) is really an art. Much like the painter mixes colors over and over until the desired hue is achieved, advanced Googlers blend the tools together in a variety of ways until quality results are achieved. Rarely do the best results come from one search attempt. This is particularly true in genealogical search because there are so many factors involved when it comes to searching for our complex ancestors.

Google's Search Index: Caffeine

It's important to understand that when you search with Google, you are not searching the live web. At first glance this may sound like a negative, but consider this: When you find a very large genealogy reference book at the library, would it be more effective and efficient to thumb through the hundreds of pages in the book, or flip to the back of the book and look through the index for what you need? Thumbing through the text would be extremely time-consuming, and that is true for Google too. Speed is a big part of why Google is so popular and so effective. Rather than "thumbing through" the vast number or webpages live, Google is able to search its index of webpages that it has already reviewed and catalogued, and do so with lightning speed.

In order to create this index, Google "crawls" the web 24 hours a day, 7 days a week indexing websites. This includes not just words, but also images, videos, links and any other types of content found on webpages. By doing this, Google learns not only what is on each website, but it creates a sort of profile of what that website is all about contextually.

In early June 2010 Google announced the completion of a new web indexing system called Caffeine. According to the folks at Google, "Caffeine provides 50 percent fresher results for web searches than our last index, and it's the largest collection of web content we've offered...you can now find links to relevant content much sooner after it is published than was possible ever before." Considering the speed with which content is being added to the web and the wider variety of content (videos, blogs, images, etc.) available, this should prove to be a big bonus.

The old index was made up of layers that revisited websites and refreshed the Google index at different rates. The top layer refreshed every couple of weeks, while the bottom layer had a fairly significant delay.

Caffeine, on the other hand, analyzes smaller chunks of the web constantly and adds them to the index right away. This method should provide a more consistently updated Google index and faster access to you as the end user.

One of the areas where you may see an improvement is in your genealogical Google Alerts (which we will cover in more detail later in this book). Since Google is delivering a fresher index more quickly, Google Alerts should be able to deliver the searches you have set up to your email inbox more quickly.

Finally, to put Caffeine's ability to index webpages into perspective, consider Google's description of its enormous scale: "Every second Caffeine processes hundreds of thousands of pages in parallel. If this were a pile of paper it would grow three miles taller every second. Caffeine takes up nearly 100 million gigabytes of storage in one database and adds new information at a rate of hundreds of thousands of gigabytes per day. You would need 625,000 of the largest iPods to store that much information; if these were stacked end-to-end they would go for more than 40 miles."

Google's goal was to have Caffeine be a "robust foundation" that makes it possible for them to build an even faster and more comprehensive search engine. They also wanted a search engine that can grow as the Internet grows while still delivering the most relative searches possible. This goal implies that we will want to keep our eye on Google because even more improvements are on the horizon.

CHAPTER 1
Search Tools

In addition to the new Caffeine indexing system, Google is regularly making changes to the Google search results page, particularly when it comes to search tools. In fact, with the rate of technological change, Google may look different from the images below. Therefore, the important thing to keep in mind is that first and foremost we are talking about search principles here, rather than exact placement of the tools. If you don't see something where it appears in my screen shots, you will at least know what you are looking for, and you can then locate it in your current version of Google.

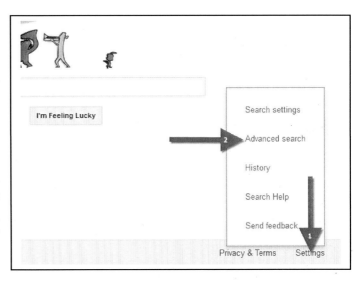

Start Your Search

Currently, you must first search for something before the various search options and tools become available on your screen. However, if you feel like you need help from the start, click Settings (*image right*) and select Advanced Search. This page (*image below*) will provide you with many options for fine tuning your search query.

In most cases though you will likely start by typing a few keywords in the Google search box, and press the Enter key on your keyboard. The next screen will reveal the results of your search, and include the very handy Search Tools (*image below*) which are dedicated to helping you quickly refine your search and achieve more targeted results.

When we enter into a new area of our genealogical research we often need to get our bearings by evaluating what's available online, as well as learn more about the nature of the records we are looking for and their place in history. For example, let's say that we want to learn more about immigration, and specifically Ellis Island passenger lists. Here's how the results page will look when we click the SEARCH button:

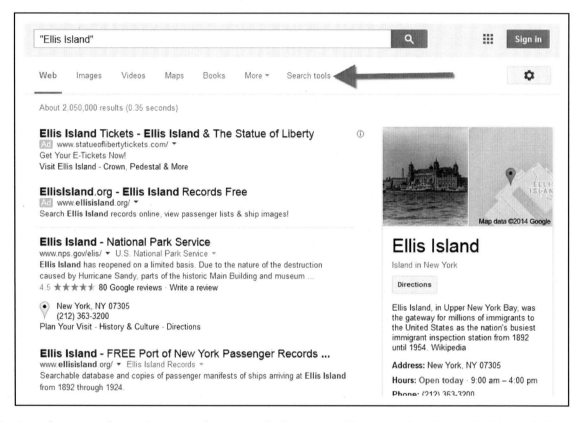

Notice the search options at the top of the page (*image above*). As indicated by the underlined word Web in this row of tools, our current search results (all 2,050,000 of them!) cover all areas of the web. However, we now have links to narrow our search by Images, Videos, Maps, Books, and More. To reveal more options, click the down arrow next to the word MORE, and a wider range of search options are now a click away.

Also in this row is the Search Tools button. This button provides further refining tools based on which search option you are using.

Images
Image search tools isn't new, but remains one of the most powerful and underutilized options in Google. Why is it so powerful? In our case using Image search would allow us to quickly assess visually which of the websites in the results list actually contains digitized passenger lists, photos, and other types of images. Depending on what you are looking for, a visual search can really speed up the process.

If we click Images on our *"Ellis Island"* search results page, the results convert to exclusively images. Clicking the Search Tools button now provides tools for further refining of the image results. You can search by size or color, which can be very helpful if you are looking for something specific to match a project on which you are working. Under the heading of Type you will find tools that will zero in on images of:

- Faces
- Photos
- Clip Art
- Line Drawings
- Animated

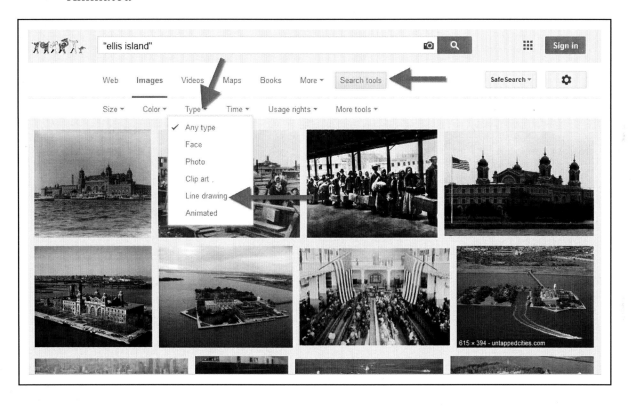

So for example, if you are looking for passenger lists associated with immigration through Ellis Island, you can quickly weed out faces and photographs by clicking on Line Drawing.

When you find a passenger list in the Line Drawing Results, click it to retrieve a full size listing for the image (*image next page*). Here you can click the Visit Page button to view the webpage where the image resides, or click the View Image button to retrieve the full size image where it is hosted on the web. You'll also see listed here the URL of the website, and the size of the image in pixels.

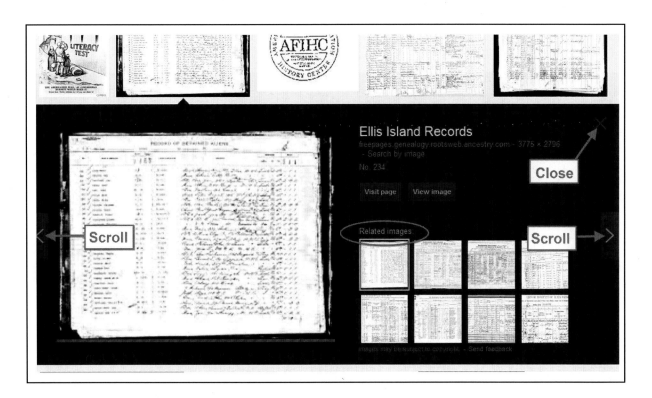

Notice the additional thumbnail images, all of which look like passenger lists. These are "Related Images" and are provided by Google based on your selection of this particular passenger list image. Google can differentiate between the types of line drawings that came up in the original image search, and deliver up those that are most closely "related" to the one you selected. This gives you quick access to the other websites that also host digitized passenger list images.

Finally, notice that there are arrows on the left and right sides of the result above. This is because this is 'image viewer' mode, and the arrows allow you to scroll through the image results one at a time. With each image Google will serve up a new collection of related images and their website origins.

To get back to the comprehensive image search results, click the "x" in the upper right corner of the image viewer.

Video

If you are looking specifically for a video about Ellis Island, the Videos search option is the link to click. Here you'll find everything - movie trailers, historic film footage, other genealogists' trips to Ellis Island, first-hand accounts by Ellis Island immigrants, and more. Click the Search Tools button and another assortment of options geared specifically to videos appears. Try clicking the drop down menu

next to Any Source and selecting different sources to see how the results change. (*Image previous page*)

Video is a fascinating way to add historic context to your research and even connect with others who may be interested in the same research areas. (For more on videos, and specifically YouTube, jump to Chapter 12.)

Maps

Planning a trip to Ellis Island? Click on the Map link and you'll be transported to Ellis Island on Google Maps.

We'll talk more about maps specifically in later chapters. However, you may not want to use the modern day map of Ellis Island, but rather you may want to look for vintage maps. Here's how:

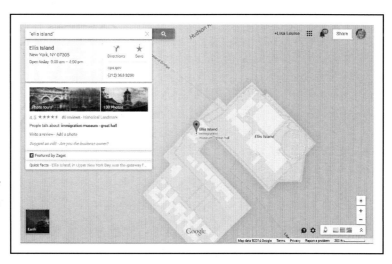

At Google (in Image search mode) type *"ellis island" historic maps* in the search box and press Enter. The results will be from a variety of websites across the web.

Click to select an historic map, and all related images will also be vintage.

Blogs

Unfortunately over the years a few search options have been eliminated from the pick list, even though they are still available. One of those is Google's Blog Search at http://www.google.com/blogsearch.

Genealogists all over the world are blogging about their research, ancestors, and genealogical interests. By conducting a Blog search for keywords that are applicable to your genealogy research, you will discover bloggers talking about what interests you. Try a blog out, and if you like it, you can subscribe to it for free. That way, up to date information will be sent automatically to you via email or through your favorite blog reader.

Expanding Your Horizons

If you would like to learn how to blog about your family history watch the four part video series "How to Blog Your Family History" at the Genealogy Gems YouTube Channel: http://tinyurl.com/genealogyblogging

Books

The vast collection at Google Books is just one click away with the Books link. We'll cover Google Books in depth in chapter 9. But for right now, here's a little tip on how to grab full length, digitized, free books quickly through search: Click Books and then click the Search Tools button and select Any Books. From the pick list click "Free Google ebooks" and all

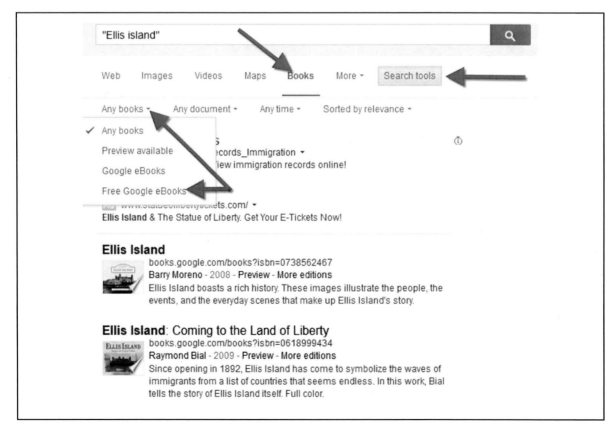

free books featuring your search term will be served up in the results.

VIDEO: *Searching for Your Ancestral Roots (with Google Books)*
http://www.youtube.com/watch?v=UwnbCmVrISQ

Related Searches
Sometimes you aren't exactly sure what you are looking for or don't realize that there are other related websites that might be helpful to your research. This is where Related Searches comes in. Scroll to the bottom of the search results page to see if Google has found searches related to what you searched for. If you find one that looks potentially useful just click that link to retrieve those results.

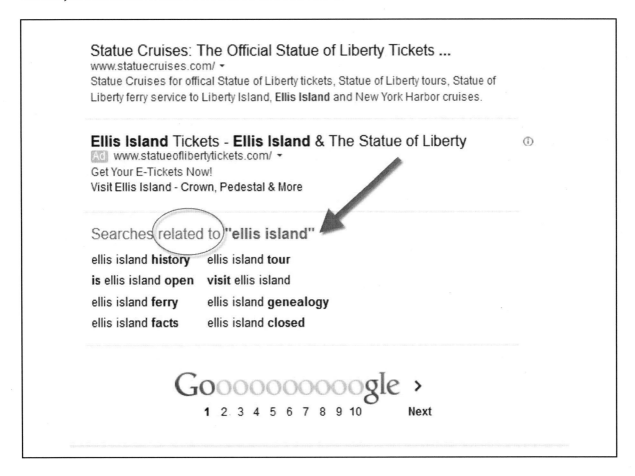

We will discuss Related Searches further in the next chapter.

CHAPTER 2
Basic & Advanced Search

Before We Start
Understanding core Google search techniques can take you a long way in your research. Once you master the basics, you can then add additional strategies that will help with your specific avenue of research.

There are two things you need to keep in mind as you conduct Internet searches:
1. **What you want may not be out there.** No matter how good the search strategies are, Google can't find what's not on the web.
2. **The web is changing moment by moment.** What isn't there now could be posted five minutes from now.

Search Basics

Keep it Simple
Even though there are some great advanced search techniques, they won't apply to all of your searches. In fact, according to Google, advanced strategies are generally only needed about 5% of the time. The percentage may be higher for us as researchers because we are trying to locate specific information about our ancestors, and we want to discern between people with the same names. However, the "Keep it Simple" principle usually applies. Google is designed to be most effective with simple, concise search queries. If you're looking for a particular business that your ancestor worked for, just enter the name, or as much of the name as you know. If you're looking for a particular concept, place, or product, start with the name.

If you're looking for a county court house, simply enter *county courthouse* and the name of the county or the zip code. Most queries do not require advanced operators or unusual syntax. Simple is definitely a good way to start.

Here are some basic guidelines to remember as you search:

1. *Every word matters*. In general all the words you put in the query will be used, with a few exceptions.

2. *Search order matters.* This has grown in importance since the first edition of this book. According to Google's Search Anthropologist Daniel M. Russell, "in the English language word order matters a lot...so when you are not getting the results you seek, try shifting the order of the words a bit." The frequency and distribution of bigrams (two words commonly found together such as *ellis island*, or *family tree*) are commonly used by many applications for simple statistical analysis of text,

and that's essentially what Google is doing. Run a search on family tree and then on tree family and you'll see that you get different results.

For a quick, easy to understand example of this watch:
VIDEO: *Word Order Matters*
http://youtu.be/xcUuNORncN0

3. ***Search is never case sensitive***. It doesn't matter whether you type "los angeles" or "Los Angeles." Go ahead and save the time it takes to shift and stick to lower case.

4. ***Punctuation is generally ignored*** by Google search. This means you can't search on special characters such as %^&()=+[]\ .

STRATEGY #1: Imagine It and You Will Find It

As a genealogist you can probably imagine how another genealogist might record data about your ancestor on a webpage. That's a big advantage when it comes to search. A search engine isn't human - all it can do is match words in your query with words on a page. Genealogists tend to use certain words when recording genealogical data and that terminology is what you should be including in your query.

For example, a non-genealogist might type in a search box:

What is the birthday of George Washington Carver?

"Birthday" is not the term a genealogist or a records website would likely use on their web page. Therefore, using that word would probably bring up all kinds of pages that fail to deliver the type of genealogical data you seek.

Instead, as a genealogist you might want to use the following search:

George Washington Carver born died
or
George Washington Carver birth death

Again the strategy here is to use the kind of words that the author of the kind of page you would be interested in would use.

STRATEGY #2: Use Descriptive Words

The more targeted and unique the words are that you use in your query, the better results you will receive. Words like 'document,' 'info,' and 'website' are generally unnecessary. Again, the idea is to think like the person who has the information that you want on their website. Ask yourself: "What words would they use?"

Rather than searching:

What does the number next to the occupation code mean in the census?

Which results in 17.5 million haphazard results, try:

Column 26D 1930 census meaning

This delivers around 56,400 results and the first 10 look like they will most certainly be able to answer the question. (*Image below*)

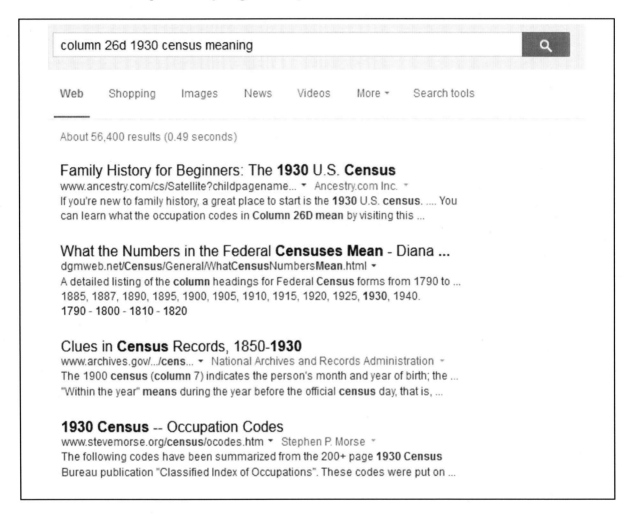

STRATEGY #3: Pull It All Together – Simple, Imagined, and Descriptive Searches

Keep it simple by using as few words and terms as possible. Each word you choose to add to your query should focus the query even more. Keeping it simple also means not focusing yourself out of results because your query has become too narrow. Since Google uses the words you search on, each additional word you add to your query will further limit the results.

This is where "imagining" comes in. Search is not an exact science because there's no way to really know what might be out there that would be helpful to your research. Simplicity leaves room for the gems you might not have known were available.

www.GenealogyGems.com

STRATEGY #4: Use Multiple Searches
Excellent search results are rarely achieved with just one click of the search button. Start by using a limited number of search words, and then add to them to focus in on your target. If a particular word or phrase seems to not be hitting the mark, try something different.

You might want to start with a search such as:

Harold Carter birth Springfield

When the results indicate there are dozens of "Springfields" around the country, you would then add:

Harold Carter birth Springfield Ohio

From there you can begin to add search operators to further clarify your query.

Search Operators
Search operators are terms that can help you further narrow or broaden your search. They explain to Google what operation you want to conduct with the keywords you include in your query.

Operator: OR
You may already be familiar with the common Boolean search operator *OR*. You can use this in your Google searches to provide for more options in the results. For example, you may not be sure whether Great Grandmother Smith is buried in Manhattan or Brooklyn. Here's how to search for cemeteries in either city:

*Cemeteries Manhattan **OR** Brooklyn*

Operator: Minus Sign (-)
Search operators can also be symbols (which is another reason why symbols aren't searchable as we discussed previously.) There are two that are used quite often, and fall in the *Basic Search* category. The first is the minus sign (-).

Let's say that you are searching a Harold Carter from Springfield, Ohio and there happens to be a prominent man named Harold Carter from Springfield, Missouri who keeps popping up in your search results. By using the minus sign operator you can sweep Mr. Carter from Missouri out of the way and off your results page.

First search: *Harold Carter birth Springfield Ohio*

Revised search: *Harold Carter birth Springfield Ohio –Missouri*

Notice that the minus sign is touching the word it is subtracting. This is critical to search success. When a search operator is telling Google to do something to a word or phrase, it must touch it, with no spaces.

The minus sign is particularly effective when you are searching for common surnames. For example, you might be searching for the surname *Lincoln* in *Missouri* but you don't want to get inundated with results for *Abraham Lincoln*. You could search on:

Lincoln –Abraham Missouri

The word *Lincoln* will be returned in your search results. Pages that include the name *Abraham* will not be included in the search results. This operator works extremely well for eliminating a word that is commonly linked to your search term but has no bearing on your research.

Operator: Quotation Marks (" ")
In the past (and in the first edition of this book) the plus sign (+) was used to make a word mandatory in a search query. However, with the advent of Google's social network Google+ the plus sign has taken on a whole new meaning. So from here on out, strike the plus sign from your searches!

When you want to accomplish what the plus sign used to do for your searches, use quotation marks. Using quotation marks around a phrase has always been a Google search technique for ensuring that exact phrase appears on each and every result. Now, the same goes for individual words that you want mandated. For example:

"U.S. Federal Census"
returns websites featuring that exact phrase, and no variation.

"Jehu Burkhart"
returns only webpages that include the exact name *Jehu Burkhart* somewhere on the page. But don't forget what we discussed earlier in this chapter in strategy #1. Always consider how the folks that are creating the webpages you seek will phrase information. It's very possible that a genealogist posting a list of revolutionary war ancestors might list them as follows:

Burkhart, Jehu
If this is the case, then the search *"Jehu Burkhart"* will not return that webpage in the results list! The lesson here is to be careful not to inadvertently eliminate results by trying to be too specific.

How might you solve this dilemma? **Mix and match search operators!**

"Jehu Burkhart" OR "Burkhart, Jehu"

As you gain skill and confidence in your searches, you will find yourself mixing and matching operators more and more. And that leads us to the Advanced Search.

Advanced Search

After you've exhausted the basic search techniques, it's time to shift into high gear with Advanced Search. These techniques will help you search with more precision and achieve even better results.

Operator: Asterisk (*)
Sometimes the words that you are looking for won't appear next to each other even though they normally do. For example, you may be looking for a city directory, and normally you would expect to see the two words together as a phrase: *city directory*. By using an asterisk to set them apart, you may find the perfect result that searching for them with quotation marks alone may have missed.

*"city * directory"*

Results could then include:
- City phone directory
- City telephone directory
- City and county directory

The asterisk is essentially a place holder, holding a spot open for a word or two. It can also be used to make room for a possible middle initial or middle name, which comes in very handy in genealogical searches!

*Lars * Larson*

Results could then include:
- Lars Larson
- Larson Johan Larson
- Lars J. Larson

Operator: Tilde (~) aka Synonym Search (Discontinued)
In the past you could use the tilde to ask Google to search for the synonym of a work. Sadly, this search operator has been discontinued. So rather than searching for...

~train history

search for

Train railroad locomotive history

This will essentially accomplish the same thing. Notice that I didn't include quotation marks around any of the synonyms that so that all can be equally considered by Google. (*Image next page*)

TOP TIP: Because of the volume of content on the web, most searches will bring more results than you could ever have time to review. But the goal is not to achieve a *very* small number of results. Rather, our goal is to deliver a smaller number of websites where the very best results possible appear on the first page or two. I like to refer to this as the cream rising to the top of the pail. And one way to help that cream rise is to simply add the word

genealogy

to your family history related searches! That way, Google knows that when choosing between a website that is talking about genealogy (or family history, ancestry, etc.) and a non-genealogical site, the genealogical site should rise to the top of the list.

Numrange Search
If ever there was a search technique made for genealogists, the *numrange* search is it!

A Numrange search allows you to retrieve results containing numbers in a given range. Just type in to the search box two numbers, separated by two periods with no spaces, along with your search terms. This is ideal for searching when you are unsure of the exact year, or want to narrow the field. For example:

George Crandall 1850..1860

Notice that each search result (*image right*) has a year bolded that

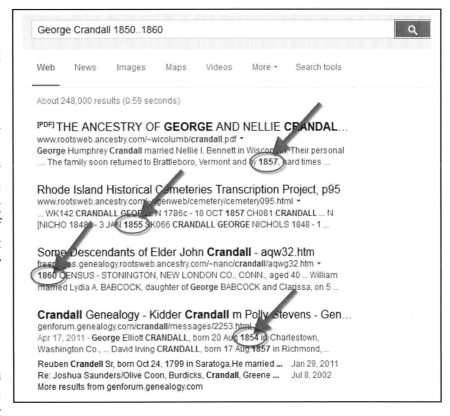

falls within the range of numbers specified in the search query. Google is telling you exactly why you received this result! By the way, Google is technically finding numbers, so don't bother adding a month or day to the date to the search!

Link Search

Let's say that you find a terrific genealogy website all about your specific family line. Wouldn't it be nice to know who else out there on the web is also interested in that family line? It would make sense that other websites that are linking to that genealogy website would be excellent candidates for further investigation.

As I said earlier, Google is constantly crawling websites in order to index the content. One of the things it is indexing is the websites that are linking to each site. Even the website owner may not know who has linked to their site, but Google does!

The Link Search empowers you to ask Google for a results list of websites that link to a given address.

For instance, if you found a great website about your saxophone-playing uncle on the *Crandall Family Web Site*, you could try the following search:

link:www.crandallfamilywebsite.com

Note there can be no space between the "link:" and the web page's homepage URL. Also, the results list is a representative sample, but does not include every single link.

The results now show web pages that are linking to www.familysearch.org: (*Image below*)

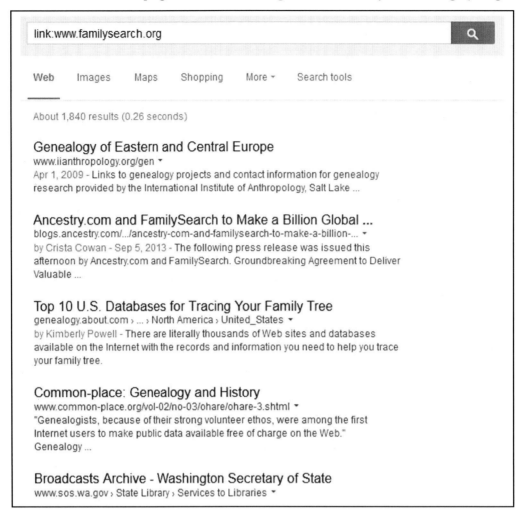

Rather than always starting from scratch with your searches, why not go after websites that have already shown a distinct interest in the subject matter you have already identified on a particular website. This would be a good time to check those web browser bookmarks you have saved over the years, and see if any of the websites warrant this type of search. The results could be exciting indeed!

Related Search
Of course, websites that discuss the same family lines will not always be aware of each other, and therefore may not be linking to each other. Related search can get around that situation.

Similar to the Link Search, the Related Search will retrieve websites that are similar, or "related" to a specified web site. The similarities are based on the index Google has created while crawling the website. If the words "Crandall," "genealogy," and "Ohio" are the most commonly used words on the *Crandall Family Website*, Google will return results featuring websites that also use those words more than any others. It will also look at whether the websites tend to link to the same online resources, and feature images with similar meta data, etc.

For example: the following search will retrieve websites that are the most similar to the *Crandall Family Website*:

related:www.crandallfamilywebsite.com

Again, there can be no space between the "related:" and the webpage URL. This is because you are telling Google to do something specifically to this website address. If you were to put a space between "related:" and the address, Google would ignore the colon, and simply use the word "related" as a keyword to search.

Also, it's important to use the homepage URL, rather than a page within the website. If you've been clicking around to various pages in the website, be sure to return to the homepage before copying the URL.

The Related Search is an incredibly powerful search tool. It's like putting an entire website that you have already confirmed is discussing your family tree in the Google search box! In fact, if you have your own family history website, that would be the perfect candidate for a Related Search.

Allintitle Search

If you start a search with *allintitle:* Google will restrict the results to only pages that have all of the search words in the title. For example, to get only documents which contain *Minnesota*, *railroad*, and *history* in the title:

Allintitle: Minnesota railroad history

With this type of search (*image right*) it is acceptable to have a space after "Allintitle:" because this operator is being applied to everything that follows it. In fact, the truth is, with or without the space, it works. And that's a good point to remember. When in doubt about spacing, try it both ways and the results will reveal whether what you are doing is working.

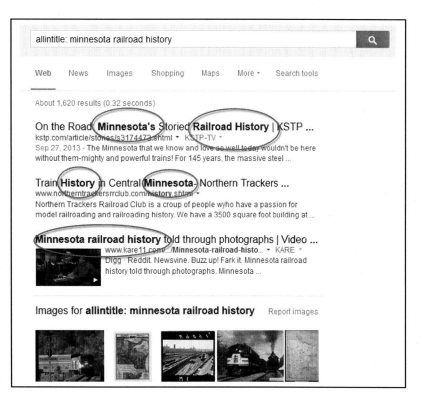

Allinurl: Search

Have you ever tried to remember a website address for a genealogy website, and although you couldn't remember the exact address, you recalled some of the keywords? If you start a search with *allinurl:* Google will restrict your search results to only those websites that have all of the search words in the URL.

For example, if an ancestor worked for the Oregon Pacific railroad and you knew that the words Oregon and Pacific were in the URL, you could do a search on:

Allinurl: Oregon Pacific

And the results page would include the Oregon Pacific Railroad Company website at http://www.oregonpacificrr.com.

As we discussed previously, punctuation and symbols are generally ignored by Google. Therefore, *Oregon/Pacific* will ignore the slash and give you the same result as no slash at all.

Quick Definition Search
Have you ever come across a word in your research and you were unsure of its meaning? For example, you see the word "cooper" in the occupation column of the census, but you don't recall what a cooper does. Simply type the following in the Google search box:

define:cooper

With one click of the Search button you'll have the answer: *a craftsman who makes or repairs wooden barrels or tubs.*

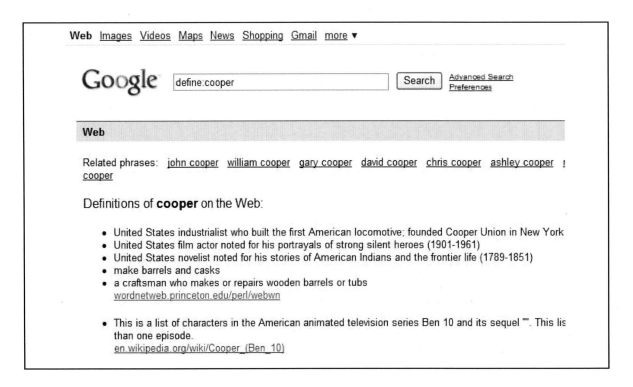

And again, there is no space between *define:* and *cooper* because we are asking Google to do something specifically with the word *cooper*. That is, define it.

If You are in a Hurry...

If these techniques seem like a challenge to remember or you're in a hurry, try Google's Advanced Search page. You'll find Advanced Search by clicking Settings on Google's homepage. You can also get there directly by going to: http://www.google.com/advanced_search.

At the Advanced Search page you will find additional search options:

Language: Specify in which language you want your results.

Date: Restrict your results to the past 3, 6, or 12-month periods.

SafeSearch: Eliminates adult sites from search results.

Search Recap

Key Concept: Keep it Simple
Less is more when it comes to search. Start simple and then revise your search to follow the right path.

Key Concept: Use Your Imagination
Think like someone who would post a webpage with the kind of information you want. Think like a genealogist for charts and reports, think like a railroad historian for background information on the railroad your grandfather worked for, and think like a librarian when searching for books.

Key Concept: Use Focused, Descriptive Words
The bottom line: each word should pack a search punch!

Key Concept: Try a Variety of Searches
Remember: "search strategies" is a plural phrase and implies that a number of searches need to be conducted to get the best results.

Key Concept: Don't Stop At a Great Website
When you find a helpful website, before you leave you have two more searches to do:

Related: Search
Link: Search

These two searches may reveal another great website you might have missed on the same topic.

CHAPTER 3
Search Strategies for High-Quality Results

The best way to illustrate the process of incorporating advanced search strategies is through examples that tackle the most common challenges.

Challenge #1: Too Many Low-Quality Results
Search Goal: Locate enumeration district maps for Sibley County, Minnesota for the available census years.

Here's the typical keyword-packed search:

Search #1: *enumeration district map sibley county*
Results: 6,080

One of the problems with such a search is that Google is looking for webpages that include any combination of the keywords. Several refer to a person with the last name "Sibley" in a "county" in another state! This is where operators come in to play. We need Google to only search for "Sibley county" rather than "Sibley" and "County" randomly on the page. To do this we use our first tool: quotation marks.

Search #2: *enumeration district map "Sibley County"*
Results: 1,240

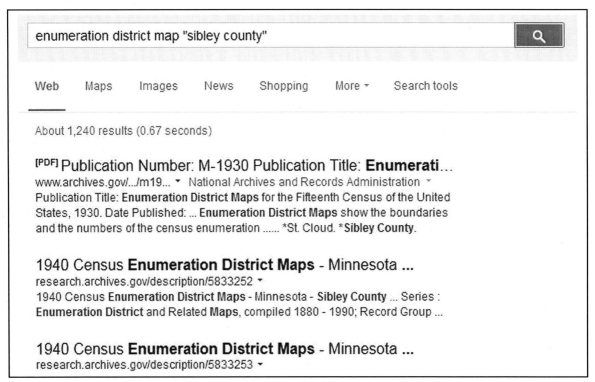

These simple quotation marks alone eliminated 4,840 results that were not specifically for Sibley County! It is a vast improvement, but just the beginning. Since we are in search of an "enumeration district" map and not just any mention of "enumeration" and "district," our next step is to apply quotation marks to those key words.

Search #3: *"enumeration district" map "Sibley County"*
Results: 509

> "enumeration district" map "sibley county"
>
> Web   Maps   Images   News   Shopping   More ▾   Search tools
>
> About 509 results (0.40 seconds)
>
> [PDF] Publication Number: M-1930 Publication Title - National ...
> www.archives.gov/.../m19... ▾ National Archives and Records Administration ▾
> Publication Title: **Enumeration District Maps** for the Fifteenth Census of the United
> States, 1930. Date Published: ... **Enumeration District Maps** show the boundaries
> and the numbers of the census enumeration ...... *St. Cloud. ***Sibley County**.
>
> 1940 Census **Enumeration District Maps** - Minnesota ...
> research.archives.gov/description/5833252 ▾
> 1940 Census **Enumeration District Maps** - Minnesota - Sibley County ... Series :

Again, this is a great improvement. The description of the first result is a webpage that begins with "Enumeration District Maps." So why didn't we put quotation marks around *"enumeration district map"* in our search? We can answer that question with a question: What if the webpage said, "Here is a map of the state of Minnesota Enumeration Districts"? That result would not have appeared, and yet may have been of great value. This is where the "art" of search comes in. Be a **Search Artist** by keeping these two things in mind:

1. Think like a webpage writer.
"Enumeration District" is a recognized phrase in genealogy, and the webpage writer who is specifically talking about enumeration district maps is highly likely to use it. However, simply including the word *map* will remove all the pages that never mention maps and therefore is effective on its own. Including *map* within the quotation marks needlessly restricts pages where the writer does not use that exact phrase.

2. Keep searches as simple as possible while fine-tuning each search attempt.
Again, we can go back to our artist analogy. The artist adds just enough tint to achieve the desired result, and avoid muddying the overall color. We don't want to muddy the waters of search with needless restrictions. Each tool employed restricts results and we don't want to miss a valuable webpage. To see this in action, give it a try:

Search #4: *"enumeration district map" "Sibley County"*
Results: 2

Two results is not enough to feel confident that you got the best result. Let's stick with Search #3, which includes a manageable number of results.

While we could take the time to go through all 509 results, that would still be very time consuming. At this point take a moment and look over the descriptions of the types of web pages we are retrieving. We still see sites that may not be quite what we are looking for. The process continues.

By clicking the Images link, Google will run the same search, but for images rather than text webpages.

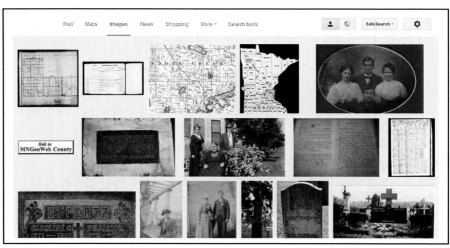

There are a few maps, but mostly photographs. This tells us something very important about what is likely not available on the internet. Digitized maps of Sibley County enumeration districts may be few and far between online. So we may want to shift our attention to locating repositories that carry such maps, which is the next best thing.

To get back to our original search, click the Web link.

Let's stop again and think like a website publisher. Enumeration districts are not limited to historic census records, and we are only interested in maps for the available historic enumerations. Therefore, there is still more whittling down that can be done on these results through continuing the search process.

We know that currently the most recent available enumeration is 1930. Let's try adding "1930" to the search to see if we can find a reference to an enumeration map for that census.

Search #5: *"enumeration district" map "Sibley County" 1930*
Results: 120

Of all of the result descriptions, the first result looks like the closest match. It's from the National Archives and refers specifically to "Enumeration District Map Sheets" associated with the 1930 census and "Sibley County." (*Image below*)

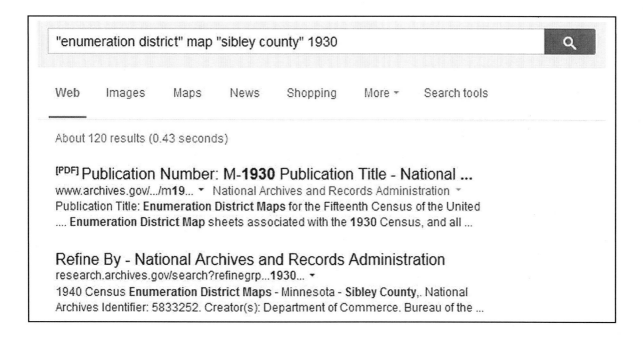

It is not a big surprise that the National Archives would be a source for such maps. However, had there been another repository that carry these maps in their collection, chances are it would also be near the top of the list. With just 120 results, looking through the first few pages (the "cream") would not be too burdensome. And again, some could be skipped all together simply from the description provided in the result.

Publication Number: M-1930

Publication Title: Enumeration District Maps for the Fifteenth Census of the United States, 1930

Date Published: 2001

ENUMERATION DISTRICT MAPS FOR THE FIFTEENTH CENSUS
OF THE UNITED STATES, 1930

Introduction

On the 36 rolls of this microfilm publication, M1930, are reproduced the Enumeration District Maps for the Fifteenth Census of the United States, 1930. These maps number some 8,345 separate sheets and they are part of the Records of the Bureau of the Census, Record Group 29. They are housed at the National Archives and Records Administration Building in College Park, Maryland.

Background

An enumeration district, as used by the Bureau of the Census, was an area that could be covered by a single enumerator (census taker) in one census period (2-4 weeks for the 1930 Census). Enumeration districts varied in size from several city blocks in densely populated urban areas to an entire county in sparsely populated rural areas. Census jurisdictions, divisions, districts, or subdivisions were used in earlier censuses and the terms "enumeration district" and "enumerator" were first used in the 1880 Census.

By clicking on the link we are taken to a PDF (*image above*), and it looks like we've hit pay dirt!

In the first paragraph we learn that the National Archives has 36 rolls of microfilmed enumeration district maps in their collection housed at the National Archives and Records Administration Building in College Park, Maryland. The next paragraph answers the question as to which census schedules have enumeration district maps: "Census jurisdictions, divisions, districts, or subdivisions were used in earlier censuses and the terms "enumeration district" and "enumerator" were first used in the 1880 census." Now we know that if we want to locate maps earlier than 1880 we need to change the keywords we use to find them.

As illustrated in this section, it is clear that the art of search is a series of steps, with each step based on the knowledge gained in the previous one taken.

QUICK TIPS
You can dig deeper into a high quality search result such as the National Archives web page we discovered by using a couple of quick tricks:

QUICK TIP #1: How to Alter the URL to Find More in Sub Directories
1. Click your mouse at the end of the URL of the current page.

2. Backspace to remove "1930.pdf" and replace it with "1920.pdf" (or the year you are looking for).
3. Press ENTER on your keyboard.

If there is a similar document available for that census year and the webmaster has uniformly created the pages, you might get lucky and very quickly get what you are looking for.

In this case we receive a page explaining that the site has been redesigned and how to locate further information. (*Image right*) However, this trick is worth a try since it is quick and easy to do.

QUICK TIP #2: How to Take a Webpage Back to Its Roots
By removing subdirectories from the URL you can quickly be taken to the main homepage for the site where you can often find the site's menu and a search box.

1. Start with the page of interest that you found in your results.
2. Click your mouse at the end of the URL.
3. Backspace to remove the portion of the address that appears after ".gov" or ".com". (*Image below*)
4. Press ENTER.

(Image above) By removing the subdirectory *microfilm* and the *m1930.pdf,* you are now in the Research area of the website where you can focus your search. (Sure enough there is a link on this page to Genealogy as well as a search box.)

Challenge #2: Researching Common Surnames
Few families escape the dilemma of surnames that are either very common, or double as common words in the English language. Here are just a few examples: Barber, Best, Booth, Church, Lemon, and West. Thankfully there are ways to refine your search to bypass the non-genealogical results clutter.

In this case study we are going to search for my husband's great grandfather, Lars Larson of Winthrop, MN. Lars was a first generation American, mayor of his town, and even served as the census enumerator in 1900.

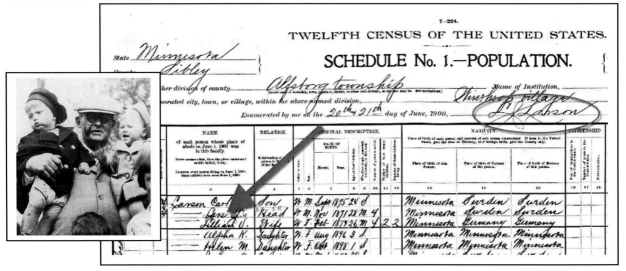

Search #1: *Lars Larson*
Results: 2,660,000! (A clear indication that this is a common name!)

The first thing that pops out from the results is that there is a radio talk show host with the name Lars Larson. In order to subtract him from the results we'll need to subtract a word associated with him that is not associated with my husband's ancestor. Some good candidates would be words like *radio* and *podcast*. The good news is that we can eliminate as many words as we wish. There's no limit to the length of your search query. Play around with your options, but be careful not to remove a word that could appear (ex. *show*.)

Search #2: *Lars Larson -radio -podcast*
Results: 1,880,000 (*Image below*)

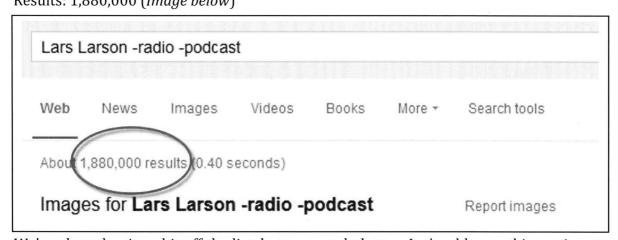

We've shaved quite a bit off the list, but we can do better. Let's add something unique to the ancestor such as the town in which he lived his entire life: Winthrop, Minnesota.

Search #3: *Lars Larson -radio -podcast Winthrop MN*
Results: 745,000

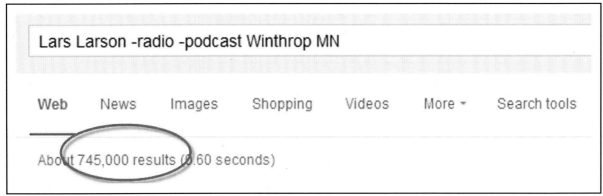

I feel pretty confident that the word "Winthrop" will appear whenever someone is talking about this particular Lars Larson. Therefore, I'm going to put the town name in quotation marks which tells Google the word must appear in all results. (*Image below*)

Search #4: *Lars Larson -radio -podcast "Winthrop" MN*
Results: 430,000

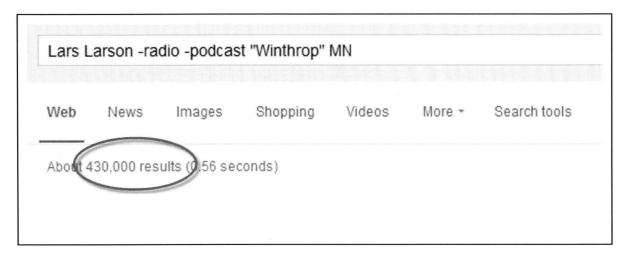

Sure enough, we almost cut the results in half. Did you notice that I used the postal abbreviation for Minnesota? Google generally understands standard abbreviations such as states, and some given names such as "Chas." (Charles) or "Thom" (Thomas).

We've come a long way from the over 2.5 million results we first achieved. There is still more fine-tuning to do. But before we go further, I would recommend clicking the various search option links that might be applicable to our genealogical search. (*Image right*) While "Shopping" may not be very helpful, under "More" we can click Google Books. (See Chapter 9 for more on Google Books.) It

would be interesting to see if any worthwhile digitized books have surfaced with the search we have conducted so far.

While Lars' name doesn't jump off the page of results, interestingly his brother's does: C. L. Larson of Winthrop, MN. (*Images below*)

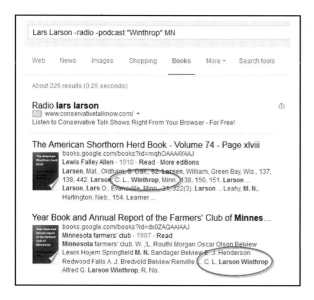
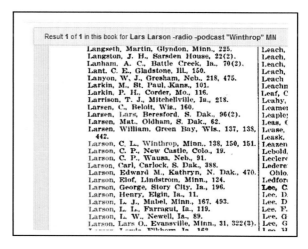

When the first result is clicked, it's clear why this book made the results list. There is a Lars Larson listed in this 1910 farming book. However, his middle initial is "O", this is not our man. However, with the yellow highlighting provided by Google, it's easy to see the "C. L. Larson" is from Winthrop, MN. A quick look at Lars' family tree confirms this is his brother, who was a farmer in Winthrop in 1910. So it's clear that Google Books has something to offer.

>### Researcher Tip:
>People often ask me, "how do you avoid going down rabbit holes like this and getting off track in your research?" We don't want to miss the opportunity to pursue this lead, but right now we are focused on Lars Larson. My solution is simple: I take a web clipping of it with the free Evernote web clipper (www.evernote.com>, and source information (in this case the URL to this book, and perhaps the books results list page as well), and add a quick note or two as to what I spotted and what I want to pursue later. Then I just tag the note with a "follow up" tag, and drag and drop it into the LARSON notebook in my Evernote library. (To learn more about using Evernote for genealogy visit my website at www.genealogygems.com and select "Evernote" from the drop down list in the "Select Content by Topic" section at the bottom of the homepage.)

Go back to the results list page on Google and click the Web link to return to standard web results. Since Lars almost always used his middle initial, I'm going to add that to the search. What the heck, let's toss some quotation marks around his name to make it exact just to see what happens!

Search #5: "Lars J. Larson" -radio -podcast "Winthrop"
Results: 4

While 4 results would usually seem a bit restrictive, these 4 are exciting because 3 of the 4 are our man! (*Image right*)

A click on the first result leads us to the Minnesota Historical Library. (*Image below*)

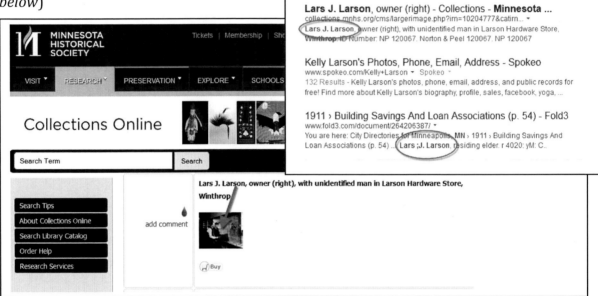

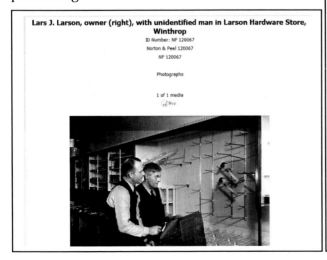

And a click on the image reveals a photograph of my husband's great grandfather Lars J. Larson working in his Larson Hardware store in Winthrop, MN! (*Image bottom left*)

Now back to the search results: (*Image bottom right*)

It appears that the second result links to the same webpage. However, the 4th result looks promising.

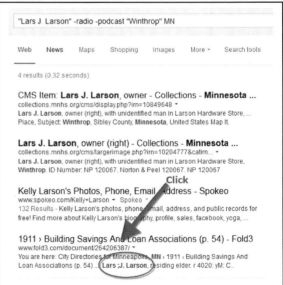

And sure enough, the genealogy records website Fold3 (*image right*) has an old newspaper that when clicked features an advertisement by Lars J. Larson! (*Image below*)

In just a few short minutes (and with a very common surname) we have zeroed in on web content that enhances our family history.

A Word about What Google *Can't* Do

Before we move on I want to make an important point about what Google CAN and CANNOT do.

Google cannot go behind password protected walls. So any webpage that requires password access can't be found in Google search.

So how did we find this item on Fold3? At the time I ran this search, the index that Google was working with of this page was actually created while this page was not password protected. Sometimes subscription websites run specials where they remove the password requirement in order to give users an opportunity to test drive them. And some websites provide digitized content initially for free, and then eventually move it behind the subscription wall.

Recently, I've noticed that subscription websites have been able to have some of their subscription content accessible to search but when you try to click through and use it, a pop up appears requiring that you purchase a subscription to gain full access. This is a smart business move because it drives more traffic to the company's website. And frankly, I believe it's good for us as genealogists as well because it makes us aware that such content is available online. And as we all know, often a subscription fee is much more economical than an airline ticket to an archive across the country.

QUICK TIP: Leave a Bread Crumb Trail

As you can see, challenging searches can take many revisions, and just as with documenting your sources, it is very important to document the search attempts you've made. As you mix and match keywords and operators, keep track of which searches steer you closest to the types of results you desire. A simple spreadsheet or table in a word processing document can do the trick. Or simply web clip the screen before you move on using Evernote, add a few comments if desired, tag as "searches" much like we discussed in the previous research tip.

Summary

In just a few minutes time we've been able to unearth a few online gems featuring Lars Larson of Winthrop, MN. Of course not every search will have such a happy ending, but if there is something out there, you are much more likely to find it using the techniques we've covered so far. We'll talk more in depth about searching for common surnames later in this book.

After working so diligently to craft the ideal search query it would be a shame to lose it. You don't have to thanks to Google Alerts. We will select your most promising search scenarios and put them to work for you in Chapter 7.

More Challenges, More Strategies

Focus on Family

Sometimes adding the word *genealogy* will aid in narrowing your search, but it depends on the surname. For example, the surname *Ward* can deliver results having to do with *hospital ward*, and *voting ward*. Generally speaking though, the addition of 'genealogy' can help move family history focused websites higher up the Google results list. Because Google has discontinued the tilde search operator for synonym search, you may also want to add words or phrases such as *family tree* and *family history*.

Famous People

Another problematic group of surnames are those shared by very famous people. If you are researching the surname Lincoln, Bush, or other prominent name then you've probably already experienced this challenge.

Use operators such as a numrange (...) to indicate a timeframe, and the minus sign to remove unwanted terms that apply to the famous person but not to your family.

Simple examples include:

John Lincoln 1845..1900 -Abraham -president

Summary

When it comes to search keep these things in mind:

- Search is an art rather than an exact science.
- There's no limit to the length of your search query.
- You can mix and match search operators.

- Track your searches to avoid confusion and duplication of effort.
- Use Evernote to save online finds for later research.
- When you can't find what you're looking for, set up Google Alerts for the most promising searches (See Chapter 7).
- Only a fraction of the available genealogy information is currently on the web, but Google searches can lead us to offline materials too.

Remember: it's just as valuable to know what is NOT available on the web (today, that is!) as what IS available on the web.

CHAPTER 4
Site Search & Resurrecting Websites

Google Site Search

How often have you found a website that looks like a prime candidate for having information about your family tree, only to discover that there is no search box available to search the site?

Without a search box, a page-by-page search would be required to locate pertinent genealogical information. Many websites contain hundreds (if not thousands) of pages, making this type of search a nearly impossible task. Thankfully, Google offers an alternative to laboriously combing through sites like these.

Google has a language for special search instructions called "syntaxes". The syntax **Site:** instructs Google to deliver only search results from the website that you specify.

Site Search Syntax

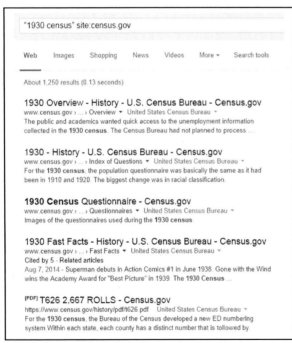

For example, the query *"1930 census" site:census.gov* will return pages that mention the 1930 census exclusively from the U.S. Census Bureau website at www.census.gov. (*Image left*) Notice also that there is no space between site: and the website address. As with search operators, this is because we are instructing Google to do something with a specific site.

It is a good practice to just copy and paste the URL from the original website to be searched in order to ensure there are no typos. However, if you're in a hurry and know the address you can type it in without

including *www*. (*Image right*)

You can also specify an entire class of websites with Site search. For example,

"1930 census" site:.gov

will return results only from websites with a .gov domain.

As with all Google searches, you can mix and match search operators with your keywords and syntax searches in order to focus your search of that specific website.

Sample Search
One of the best ways to understand the power of the site search and how it works is by test-driving it.

You are probably familiar with the U.S. GenWeb Project at http://www.usgenweb.org. It's a very popular free genealogy website run by volunteers all over the country. Information is arranged by state and then by county. Because each county website is created and maintained by volunteers, no two counties are set up exactly the same. It is not uncommon to find a large county website that does not have a search box.

Remember Great Grandpa Lars Larson from the previous chapter? Let's say that I am interested in finding all Larsons from the town of Winthrop and the surrounding area within the county on the Sibley County USGenWeb website. Although the Sibley County website has many pages and voluminous information, it does not have a search box. This means that I would have to search page by page for the surname Larson. However, Site search provides a quick and easy way for me to search the site using Google.

How to Search a Specific Website:
1. Go to http://www.usgenweb.org.
2. Click on Minnesota.
3. Click Minnesota Counties.
4. Click on Sibley. You will be taken to the Sibley county GenWeb Project website. As you can see there are a lot of links and databases listed, but no search box.
5. Click on the URL for the home page of the site to highlight it.
6. Copy the address by pressing the Control and C keys on your keyboard, or right-clicking and selecting Copy.
7. Go to www.Google.com.
8. In the search box type *"Larson" SITE:*.

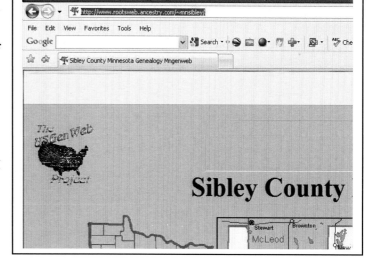

9. Immediately after the colon, paste the URL you copied by pressing the Control and V keys, or by right-clicking and selecting Paste.
10. Click the Google Search button.
11. The results page includes pages that include *Larson* only from the Sibley County USGenWeb site. (*Image next page*)

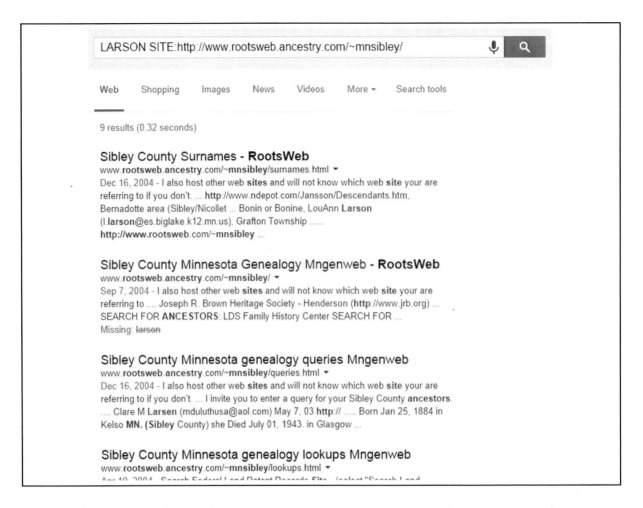

Think of the possibilities! Surnames, town names, names of businesses where your ancestors worked - the results are focused on *your* research needs!

As with all searches, you can employ all of the search strategies and operators. For example, if I had received a large number of results, I might want to revise my search as follows:

"Larson" "Winthrop" site:http://www.rootsweb.ancestry.com/~mnsibley/

Notice that the website URL for the Sibley County, Minnesota US GenWeb Project site has the domain name www.rootsweb.ancestry.com. This is important to note. We started on the US GenWeb Project site, but when we clicked through to the state of Minnesota we actually left the www.usgenweb.org site and were sent to the www.rootsweb.ancestry.com web site. This means that when we conduct a site search using the address for the Sibley County, MN site, we are only asking Google to search for our keywords in that site. It will not be searching any of the www.usgenweb.org pages. In the case of this search, that is acceptable. But if you are not getting the results you expect from a site search, take a moment to make note of where you started and which domain you are actually searching. Many websites will send you to companion web sites for different content. Site search can only search one website domain (and all of the pages that site contains) at a time.

Additional Syntax Instructions

Here's a list of syntax instructions that you can use to advance your searches:

Syntax instruction	Function	Example
inurl:	Finds pages with a search word in the web address.	*Larson inurl:genealogy*
intitle:	Finds pages with a search word in the webpage title that appears in your browser.	*intitle:"Larson genealogy"*
filetype:	Limits your search to PDF, doc, ppt (PowerPoint) or other file formats. Go to http://tinyurl.com/q8vtma8 for a list of supported file types.	*genealogy filetype:ppt* will give you PowerPoint presentations with *genealogy* in the file name.
define:	Finds the definition of the word that follows. Handy for unfamiliar words and occupations that pop up in records.	*define:cooper*
site:	Applies your search query to one specific website.	*census site:lisalouisecooke.com*

Putting It All Together

By combining the techniques we've covered thus far, you can create a very strong and efficient research strategy. By using this strategy you will find you have more time to spend on reviewing quality results.

Resurrecting Websites

Have you experienced the following scenario?

You construct a great search, which provides a number of promising results. One of the results really catches your eye: it looks exactly like the kind of information you were searching for!

The catch?

When you click the link to access the page you get the following message...

"File Not Found" (*Image right*)

...and your hopes are dashed.

Or perhaps you want to refer back to an item you found previously, only to find it has been removed from the website.

Here's a little known fact: "File Not Found" doesn't necessarily mean the information is gone forever. The same goes for deleted data. You may be able to find it in the *Cache* version of the webpage.

Behind the Scenes
As you know, Google "crawls" the web constantly indexing websites. It also takes a snapshot of each page it examines and caches, or stores, the image as a backup. It's the behind-the-scenes information that Google uses to judge if a page is a good match for your search queries.

In the case of a website that no longer exists, the cache copy provides a snapshot of the website when it was still active. Practically every search result includes a *Cached* link.

How to Retrieve a Cache Webpage:
1. When you land on a "File Note Found" error page, click the Back button on your browser to return to the Google search results page.
2. Directly under the website title is the URL. Click the small down arrow right next to that address.
3. "Cached" will be one of the options presented in the pop up menu. Clicking on the *Cached* link will take you to the Google cached version of that webpage, instead of the current version of the page.

Cached versions of websites can also be useful if the original webpage is unavailable because:
- of internet congestion;
- the website is down, overloaded, or just slow. Since Google's servers are typically faster than many web servers, you can often access a page's cached version faster than the page itself; and
- the website owner recently removed the page from the web.

If Google returns a link to a page that appears to have little to do with your query, or if you can't find the information you are seeking on the current version of the page, take a look at the cached version by clicking the cached link. You will then see the webpage as it looked when Google last indexed it.

You'll notice that a gray header will appear at the top of the page. This provides you will the following information about the cached page you are viewing:

- The original web address of the page.
- The date and time that the page you are viewing was cached.
- A link to the current version of that page.

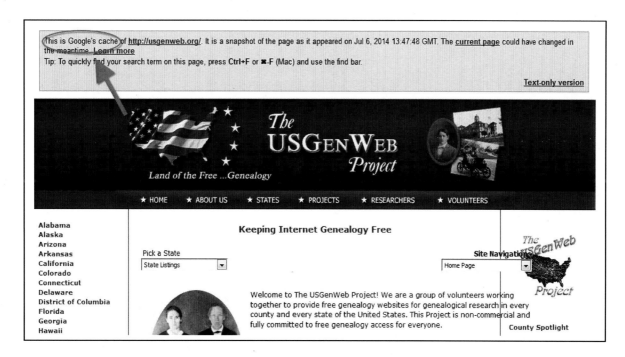

If you don't see a cached link in a search result, it may have been omitted because the website owner has requested that Google remove the cached version, or requested that Google not cache their content. Also, any sites Google has not yet indexed won't have a cached version.

Be aware that if the original page contains more than 101 kilobytes of text, the cached version of the page will consist only of the first 101 kbytes (120 kbytes for pdf files).

Summary
Before you give up on that website that appears to be long gone, _click the cache_ and you may just get lucky!

Interested in learning more about caching?
VIDEO: _HTTP Caching_
http://www.youtube.com/watch?v=MtJXwsxK7u8

CHAPTER 5
Image Search

Every day that goes by more and more images are being added to the web. What does that mean for the genealogist? It means your chance of finding a photo of one of your ancestors, or images of the events and locations associated with their lives, gets better every day. Thankfully, as the number of images on the internet increases, so does the search technology that helps you to locate them.

Since Google first introduced *Image Search* in December of 2001, users have been able to search for photos and images by the keywords in the filename of the image, the link text pointing to the image, and text adjacent to the image.

To illustrate the current breadth of available online images, Facebook has gone on the record as saying that over 6 billion images are uploaded on to their site alone every month. And Facebook images marked 'public' can be found through Google. Well, Google appears to have set its sights on being the search index that has over 1 trillion images to search from. It's inevitable that there will be a wealth of genealogical and historical images tucked into those 1 trillion images, and that's what we will be searching for in this chapter.

Conducting Image Searches

Start your image search at Google.com. The home page continues to evolve, and is currently much simpler and cleaner than in the past. If things look different when you conduct your search you can always go directly to Image search at http://images.google.com.

How to Search for an Image with Google:
1. At Google's homepage, click the Images link.
2. You will then be taken to Google's Image Search, which looks much like the classic version of Google.
3. Type keywords for the image you are looking for in the Search box.
4. Click the Search button.

www.GenealogyGems.com

Search Results will include:
- Images by type
- thumbnail size images
- the image size (hover your mouse over image to reveal)
- a link to the page on the web that contains the image (click image to access)

To find photos of specific people, try putting their first and last names with or without quotes (i.e. "George Washington"). If you are researching an ancestor's surname that is less common (i.e. Sporowski) then you would likely search without quotes in order to cast the widest net for results.

It's important to remember that image search is not limited to photographs of people. Here are some ideas for photographs worth searching that could enhance your family history research:
- Places where your ancestors lived and visited (buildings, roads, landmarks)
- Recorded events (i.e.: The Great San Francisco Earthquake of 1906)
- Cemeteries and tombstones
- Photos of heirlooms

Images are also not limited to photographs. You can use the Google image search to find:
- Maps
- Drawings
- Paintings
- Old postcards
- Charts and graphs
- Clipart

(Image below: search results for genealogy. Note the variety of images.)

Search Example

Let's say the Work Projects Administration employed one of your ancestors during the Great Depression and you want to search for images of WPA workers. Type "WPA worker" in the search box and click the Search Images button. Your results list will include many historic images related to the WPA. (*Image below*)

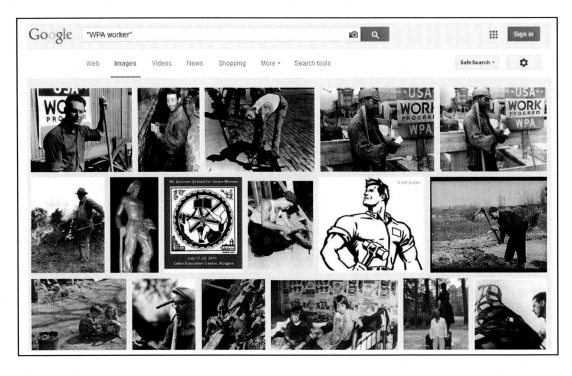

As with any Google search, all of the search operators and syntax can be incorporated to focus your image search.

Advanced Search

It's inevitable that when you do an image search, you will end up with some images that don't appear to have anything to do with what you were searching for. To address this problem, Google is incorporating some of the best Object Recognition Technology available.

> ***Object Recognition Technology*** *(from Wikipedia): Object recognition in computer vision (computer vision is the science and technology of machines that see) is the task of finding a given object in an image or video sequence.*

This technology can help you narrow down the results to meet your specifications. You can tap into this tool with Google's Advanced Search. Let's look at an example of how this works.

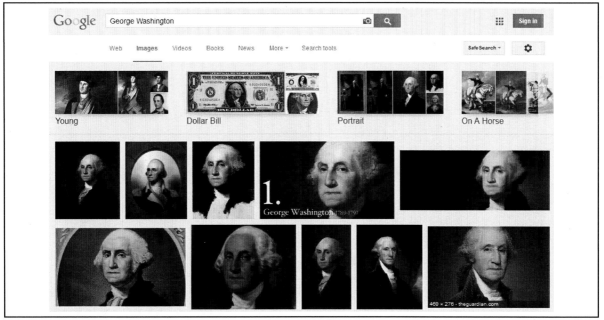

Remember our search for "George Washington"? In the results pages you will see many faces of George Washington. (*Image right*)

However, as you move on through the search results, soon you'll come across a photograph of George Washington's false teeth. Not exactly what you were looking for. (*Image below*)

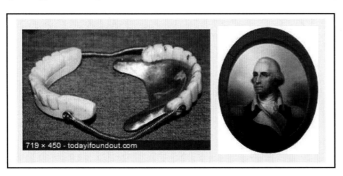

To eliminate the unwanted images and narrow in on the desired images, go back to the search box and click the Search Tools button. Fine tune the type of search by clicking the down arrow next to "Type." Using this tool you can narrow your search only to "Face".

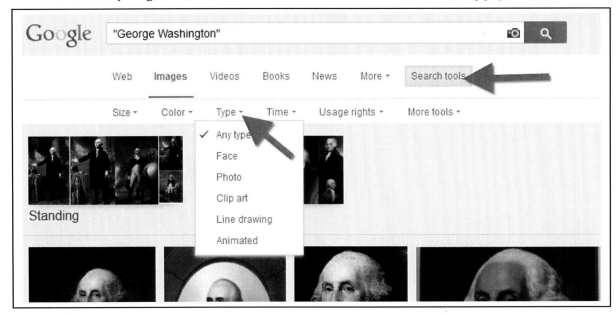

Now every search result is a facial image. It may be a portrait on a stamp or on a coin, but it will be a face. Think how well this might work with an ancestor who is not quite is famous as George Washington!

It is still possible that some of the results may not be George Washington's face. For example, the results may include an image of the face of someone who works at George Washington University because this technology has not yet been perfected. However, Google has made a commitment to start adding features that use complex image analysis. In the future, this may mean that once you have zeroed in on the face

you're looking for Google will be able to detect it specifically and narrow your results even further. This technology already exists and is currently being used by law enforcement agencies. But for now, Google has added a taste of this experience to the Google Images search box since the last edition of this book. It's called "Search by Image."

Search by Image

On the Google Images search page you'll notice that there is now a small camera icon. Click it and a special search box will pop up giving you two ways to search using actual images. The first is by URL for an image that is already posted online. The second is to upload an image from your computer. Let's give each method a try.

Image URL Example Search:

Perhaps you are fortunate enough to come across a website that refers to your ancestors and includes scanned images of post cards (*image right*) they sent to other family members. If you could identify the location shown in the postcard, it would give you a clue about where she lived or visited.

How to Search by Image:

1. Right click on the image and select "View Image." The image alone should appear in the browser window with a URL that ends in an image file extension such as .jpg.

2. Copy the URL by pressing the Control and C keys (Windows) or Command and C (Mac) on your keyboard.

3. Go to Google, and click the camera icon in the search box.

4. Paste the URL into the Google "Search by Image" box with Control V (Windows) or Command + V (Mac.) *(Image second from the top)*

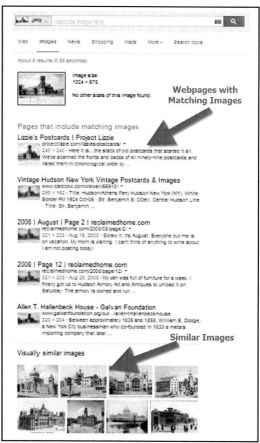

5. Click the blue search button and Google will attempt to match the image with like images on the web.

Alternative method: You can also open two browser windows, click on the image in one browser window, and drag and drop it onto Search by Image in the other. The results will look something like the image on the right.

Click a result and very quickly we have our answer as to the name and location of the building in our original image. (*Image left*)

Webpages that have included an image that matches nearly exactly will be listed. Below that will be "visually similar" images which in this case are black and white line drawings of buildings. This is an exciting new way to identify your own photos, postcards, and other vintage images.

This evolving technology offers powerful possibilities for genealogists in the future. Think of the Dead Fred website at http://www.deadfred.com. There are thousands of faces in vintage photographs on the Dead Fred website that are currently unidentified. But what if some day we could do a facial recognition search on a known ancestor and be able to pull in results of unidentified faces from other websites that match? Faces that were once unknown may turn out to be yet another portrait of one of your ancestors!

Photo *tags* can also potentially assist with identification of vintage photographs.

When we look at a vintage photo, we are often able to determine where the people in the photo were from based on the photographer's name and location on the back of the image or on the edges of a cabinet card. This was an early form of "tagging."

In today's world, this same type of information–location, names, dates– can be *tagged* onto digital photos.

In the case of images of unknown ancestor photos, we could potentially search utilizing face recognition technology in conjunction with photo information tags.

Pictures from the Past

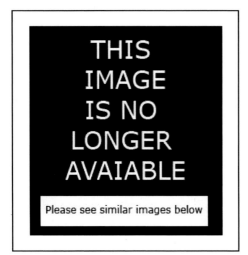

Has this ever happened to you? You conduct an image search and locate a great image that would be ideal for your research only to click on the image and get a page that says "the image is no longer available"? (*Image left*)

If you click on the thumbnail image in your search results and the image is no longer available, there may be another way to retrieve it.

As we discussed in Chapter 4, Google is constantly "crawling" the web and indexing webpages and images to include in the results of your searches. Each time a webpage or image is crawled, Google caches the page.

Because Google doesn't crawl for images as often as it does for webpages, you may find an image has moved or been removed since the last time Google indexed the website where it resided. This means you may be able to locate the missing image from the older cached version of the website.

How to Retrieve an Image that is No Longer Available:
1. Use your mouse to highlight the website's URL that appears below the thumbnail image in the search results.
1. Press Control + C on your keyboard to copy the address.
2. Click the Web link above the Google search box to go back to website searches.
3. Place your cursor in the search box by clicking inside it.
4. Press Control + V on your keyboard to paste the URL into the search box.
5. Click the Search button.
6. The first few results should be from the website that had the image you wanted.
7. Look at the last line of the result for that website and click on the *cache* link.
8. Now you are looking at a cache version of the website where the image once appeared. Browse through the site and look for the image. If you're lucky the version of the website that you are viewing was saved <u>before</u> the image was removed, and the image may still be there.

(Image Below: Paste the URL of the cached website in the web search box.)

This may sound like a lot of effort, but when only that missing image will do, you will be glad to have this little search technique in your skill toolbox.

Similar Images
In the first edition of this book I referred quite often to one of my favorite tools: Google Labs. It was a virtual playground of new ideas being explored and executed by Google. However, as we all well know, technology sits still for no one. Within six months of publication Google announced the demise of Google Labs, discontinuing many of the projects while moving the most effective ones to official Google status.

One of the "experiments" being conducted in Google Labs was Similar Images search. Thankfully it was not only retained, but has improved dramatically. Think of Similar Images search as searching for web content using pictures rather than words.

The best way to see the value in the Similar Images search is to give it a test run.

How to Conduct a Similar Images Search:

1. Go to http://www.google.com.
2. Conduct an Image search on the word *genealogy. (Image right)*
3. The results will include many familiar images like trees, charts, vintage photos, cartoons, collages, ancient artwork, and more.
4. Scroll down the results page until you find an image you like (I have selected a vintage looking family tree chart.) (*Image below*)

5. Click and drag the image you have selected to the top of the screen. A box called "Search by Image" will appear. Drop the selected image where it says "Drop image here."

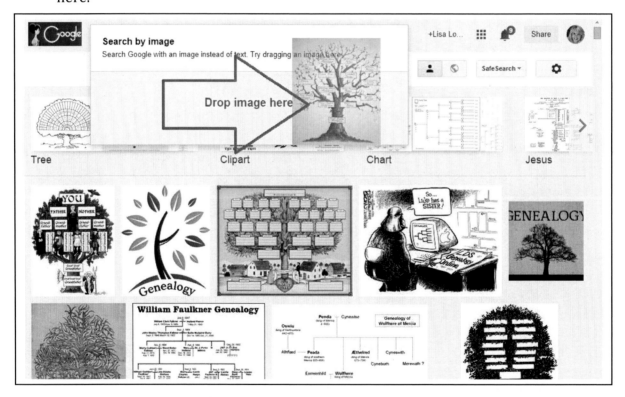

6. Instantly your results will change from a wide variety of images to results that closely resemble the image you selected. Now all of the results are similar to the one you selected, and Google has provided its best guess at the subject of the image: "genealogy tree". Notice also that the search field now displays the image being used to conduct the Similar Search.

7. Scroll down the page to the section called "Visually Similar Images." Notice that all of the images shown are similar in color and style to the one selected.

8. Click the "Visually Similar Images" link *(image right)* to receive the complete results list. (*Image below*)

The Search Tools, which can be used for further refinement of the results, now appear at the top of the list.

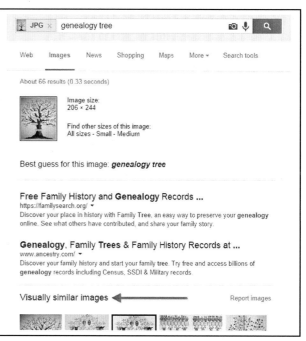

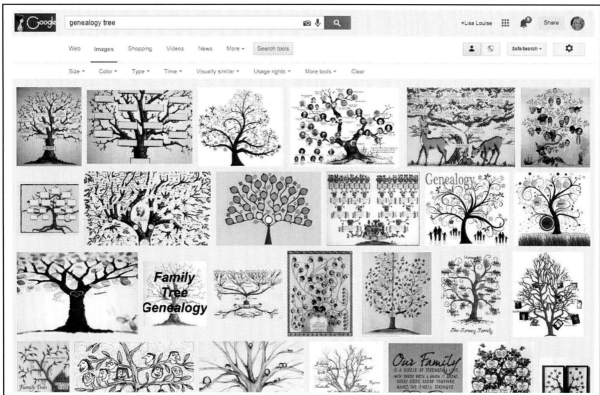

Let's look at another genealogical example.

Suppose that you've just discovered that your great, great grandfather was a blacksmith and you'd like to find a vintage image of a blacksmith for a report. You could go from website to website hoping that you'll come across a representative image that suits your needs – OR – you could run a Similar Image Search.

Conduct a Similar Images search on *Blacksmith*.

Click and drag the image that best meets your needs to the top of the page. (*Image right*) In my case, I have selected a vintage photograph of a Blacksmith inside his shop.

Now you have a number of results that all are similar in appearance and theme to the image you selected. (*Image below*) Once you find the photograph you want, you can click through to the website to determine the copyright restrictions or contact the webmaster for more information about the image.

Similar Images could be a very fast and effective tool for reviewing image options from across the internet.

TIP: Review image results more quickly by enlarging your view.
On a PC press and hold the Control key and then tap the minus sign key to the overall screen view shrinks allowing you to view more at one time. Pressing Control and the plus sign will enlarge the view, which comes in handy for small print. And finally, return to normal screen view with Control and the number zero key.

The Microphone Search Button
Did you notice that the Google search box also now includes a microphone search button next to the camera icon? This gives you yet another way to conduct a Google search!

The Microphone Button
Whether you are running an image search or a regular web search, you can now enter your search query by simply speaking to Google. The Voice Command feature is activated through

the microphone button when you are using the Chrome web browser.

To get started, you will first need to either download Chrome for free from https://www.google.com/chrome/browser/ or check for updates if you already have it by clicking the Chrome menu button (three horizontal lines) and selecting "Update Google Chrome." (*Image top right*)

Chrome Menu

Next, you need to have a microphone set up on your device. Many people prefer a headset with a microphone built in so that they can voice search completely hands free. You can also use the microphone built into your computer, or hook up an external microphone.

Once your microphone is hooked up, simply click the microphone button in the Google search box. The first time you do this, you will likely be asked to "allow" Google to use your microphone. From this point forward you no longer have to click the microphone button. Simply go to www.Google.com and say "OK Google," and ask for what you want. *(Image center right)*

genealogy gems

And as usual Google will deliver a results list. *Image bottom right)*

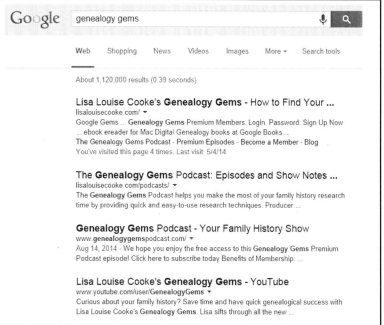

As of this second edition of the book Google Voice Command has come a long way, and yet it has a long way to go. Currently the feature only accepts words, and doesn't respond to you incorporating search operators into your command. However, who knows, by time you read this that too may be possible!

GoOgLy FUn
Remember the original Star Trek TV series?
Head to Google and say
"OK Google, Beam me up Scotty!"
The results are GoOgLy FUn!

More Image Search Tips

- If you come across a name in your genealogy research and are unsure if the first name is a man's name or a woman's name, conduct a search on that name and then click "Images" and the results will likely provide the answer to the question.

- If you don't know the meaning of a word, conduct an Image search and the resulting pictures may assist you.

- To quickly assess the contents of a website, search the images. On the Advanced Image Search page at http://www.google.com/advanced_image_search enter the address of the website that you want to search in the *Site or Domain* search box.

- When conducting Image searches, experiment with the Search Tools bar. (*Image below*) You can sort results by image size, type, color, time of posting on the web, and usage rights.

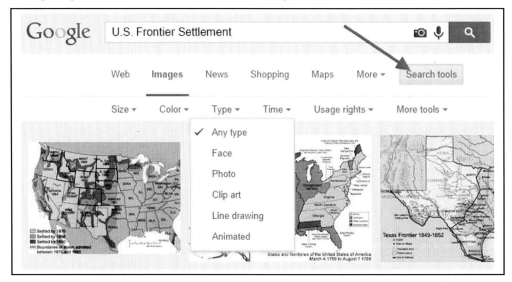

Looking to the Future

Google isn't limiting image recognition to just the faces of people. In the first edition of this book I stated that "in the future, you will be seeing an ability to find objects in photographs and use them as a reliable benchmark for filtering irrelevant images." And indeed Google has made significant strides in this area. They have developed an algorithm that has the ability to locate and label multiple objects in photographs. It was revealed at the *ImageNet Large-Scale Visual Recognition Challenge competition* (ILSVRC), the largest academic challenge in "computer vision," and each year has doubled in effectiveness. This might come in handy if you are looking for a particular landmark or item that pertains to your research.

Another feature we can expect to see more of in the future from Google is *GPS Enabled Encoding*. With 300 million digital images being snapped every day, it may prove very helpful to encode the photo with the exact geographic location where that camera phone or digital camera was located when it snapped the photo.

What could this mean for your genealogy research? In the case of an image search for an ancestor's tombstone it could make quite a difference. The author of a webpage may have neglected to give complete source information as to where the photograph was taken, or not labeled the photo in such a way that a regular Google image search would bring it up in search results. But Google may still be able to locate the image for you based on the geographic location encoded into the digital image.

And finally, Google has developed an improved algorithm for ranking images in order of their relevance to your specific search called VisualRank.

> ***VisualRank*** *is a system for finding and ranking images by analyzing and comparing their content, rather than searching image names, web links, or other text.*

We should continue to see ongoing improvements in image results. However, all of this innovation costs money. So expect to see the addition of image display ads next to image results. The good news is that you'll be more likely to come across image ads when doing queries for commercial items, rather than historic photos. Google has promised to keep ads low key to avoid detracting from the user experience.

CHAPTER 6
Common Surname Searches

In the year following the publication of the first edition of this book approximately 51 million websites were added to the Web according to pingdom.com, a website and performance monitoring company. And that is just in one year! Even without factoring for growth, we could guess from this number that the web has grown from the 634 million websites in 2011 to a number fast approaching 800 million by the end of 2014. These staggering numbers make the thought of searching for ancestors with common surnames (or surnames that double for commonly used words) on the web daunting indeed! In chapter 3 we tried our hand at searching for an ancestor with a common name. In this chapter we will delve deeper to fully equip you for success.

You're Not Alone! Everyone is Plagued with Common Surname Challenges
Within an hour of posting the question "Which surnames cause the most grief when it comes to Internet searches?" on Facebook, I received over 40 responses from family historians. They were frustrated by the surnames in their family that double as common words in the English language, and therefore double the trouble when it comes to online searching.

There's no need to let the ever bulging internet stop you from searching. In this chapter we will put into practice what we have learned from previous chapters and add new strategies that will help us zero in on the right "John Doe" among many. We will weed out irrelevant search results to save time. And, we will improve the chances that the information you post online will be found by other genealogists in their searches.

A New Ally: Google Web History
When you run a Google search, Google strives to provide the best possible results. In order to do that, they customize your search results based on your past search activity on Google with Web History. If you regularly search for genealogy topics online, this means that when you search for an ancestor with a common surname Google will give genealogy focused sites higher priority in your search results.

You must have a free Google account to take advantage of Web History, and if you have a Gmail or YouTube channel, then you already have one. You can sign in or sign up at www.Google.com/accounts.

How to Control Web History:
1. Sign in to your account.
2. Click the profile circle. (*Image right*)
3. Click "Account".
4. Click "Account History".

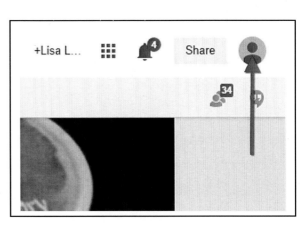

The Account History page has gone through several major overhauls since 2011, and will likely continue to evolve over time as privacy concerns continue to be addressed.

Here's the layout as of the publication date of this edition. (*Image below*)

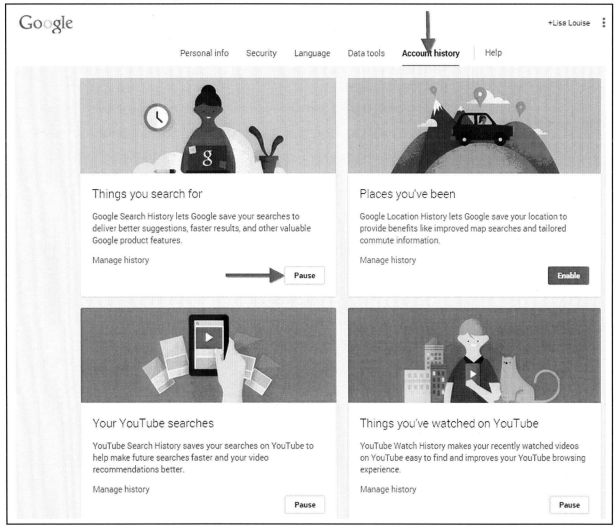

As you can see, you now have the ability to track your activity across various Google tools from your one consolidated account. (*Image right*)

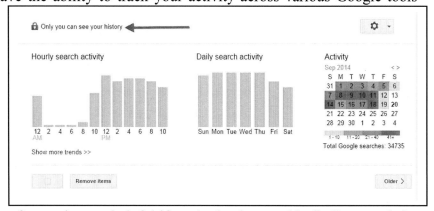

You can pause Web History at any time by simply clicking the Pause button. (*Image above*)

Click "Manage History" to see your search habits, remove items, and see your most recent searches. This last feature is very helpful if you're having trouble finding a website you want to return to. As indicated in the image on the right, only you can see your history because you are signed in to your account using your password.

You can learn more about your privacy on Google http://www.google.com/intl/en/policies/.

Now that you know how to turn Web History off, you might want to consider leaving it on in order for Google to gain a better understanding of your search habits. If you are like me, Google will learn very quickly that much of what you search for is genealogy related. Google can take this in to account as it determines how to rank your results.

The Bottom Line:
If it's been a while since you used Google to search for your more challenging surnames, go back and give it another try. The results may pleasantly surprise you.

Crafting Search Queries for Common Surnames

We are going to pull from everything we have learned so far to craft search queries that will zero in on the right person. Remember to:

- **Be a search artist by blending keywords.**
  Use the right tools (operators) and step back to analyze your results.
- **Keep in mind the "exact science" of search.**
  Google takes your query literally! If you are not getting the results you expected or hoped for, revise what you are telling Google to search for, and not to search for!
- **Think like the person who would post the information you seek.**
  Search for the terminology and word order (last name first or last name last) they would use.

The Golden Rule of Searching Common Surnames:
Search for what is Uncommon about the Ancestor with a Common Surname

When I was a kid I used to love the picture puzzles where you had to search carefully through a picture and find the very subtle differences between the two. Spotting differences between two people with the same name is not a lot different. By identifying unique features about the person you seek, you can use those to your advantage in Google search queries.

Consider keywords that might be associated with the person such as a specific location, an occupation, an unusual given name of a relative, etc. Build these elements into your search to customize it.

And keep in mind what other genealogists will be searching for when posting information online in places like message boards. This is particularly important when it comes to spelling variations.

Turn to your individual and family group worksheets for ideas. In our earlier case study we were searching for information on Lars Johan Larson. Here are some possible keywords unique to Lars that I could incorporate into a Google search:

Residence: *Winthrop, MN*
Wife: *Lillian Victoria Emmerich*

Occupations held: *Mayor, Lumber and Hardware business owner, census enumerator*
Life span years: *1871-1937*
Religion: *First Congregational Church*
Father: *Carl Johan Larson*
Unique associated names: Daughter: *Alpha*, Brother: *Swan*

No matter how utterly common you think your ancestor's name is, or the surname you are researching, the truth is every single one is as unique as a snowflake. No other Lars Larson has this combination of keywords associated with him. Take heart that even the toughest cases have loads of great keywords to work with.

Results Analysis

Internet searches rarely achieve ideal results with the first search. There's a lot to learn from search results that will improve your skills. Take time to analyze the results you receive and determine which keywords are associated with the unwanted websites. Employ the minus sign operator to remove them and run your search again. For example there is a popular radio show host named Lars Larson, so when I search for Lars J. Larson I add the following to my search query:

-radio

This helps eliminate webpages associated with the radio host from my genealogy searches. I could also add a numrange search to further define which Lars Larson I seek:

1871..1937

You will know you are really becoming a Google search expert when your search queries become longer and you run multiple versions of the query before achieving the desired results!

Once you do locate a website that mentions your common named ancestor remember to use that website to your advantage by running a Related search and a Link search as we discussed previously. This will quickly lead you to other valuable websites.

Put Google to Work for You

You certainly don't want to lose all your hard work that you have put into crafting your search queries. Rather than creating dozens of sticky notes with your searches scribbled on them, wouldn't it be nice to be able to save them and have Google search them automatically for you into the future? That's exactly what we are going to do in the next chapter with Google Alerts.

CHAPTER 7
Google Alerts

https://www.google.com/alerts

Since information is being uploaded to the web constantly, it's nearly impossible to keep up on new webpages that may contain information about your family tree. By setting up a Google Alert for the searches you have already conducted, you won't have to go out every day on the web and search to see if there is anything new. Instead, Google will do the work for you. Google Alerts is like having your own online research assistant!

Google Alerts are emails automatically sent to you when there are new Google results for your search terms. You can also have your alerts delivered to you via an RSS feed to the feed reader of your choice which we will discuss later in this chapter.

Creating Google Alerts

Here's the search query I put together for Lars Johan Larson of Winthrop, MN:

"Lars * Larson" OR "Larson Lars" "Winthrop" MN 1871..1937 –radio

I'm going to set this up as a Google Alert so that Google will search the web 24/7 for me, and only send me the best new results it finds.

How to Set Up a Google Alert for a Search:
1. Go to: http://www.google.com/alerts
   (Remember: you must be signed in to your Google account to set up alerts.)

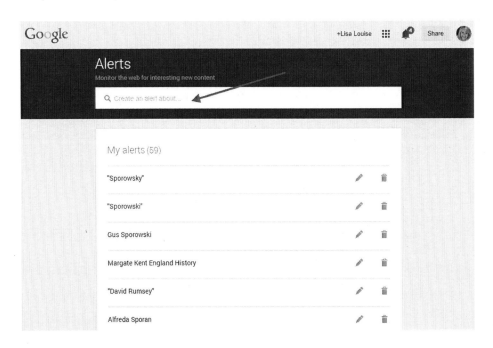

www.GenealogyGems.com

2. In the *Create a Google Alert* box type in the search terms.

   Example: *"Lars * Larson" OR "Larson Lars" "Winthrop" MN 1871..1937 –radio*

3. Click the Show Options down arrow to set up the search parameters.

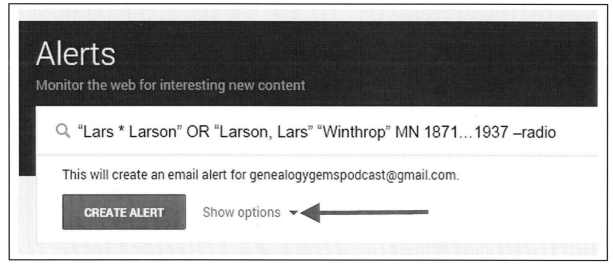

You can also select how often you want to receive search results. If you have several Google alerts or if it's a topic where there is a lot of new information being published, you may want to select to only receive one email a day, or even once a week. But you can also select receive results the moment they are found.

You can also select the type of search that you want Google to conduct. In most cases you will want to conduct an Automatic search (previously known as a Comprehensive search) which will cause Google to search all types of websites. However, there might be other occasions where you would want to select one of the other categories:

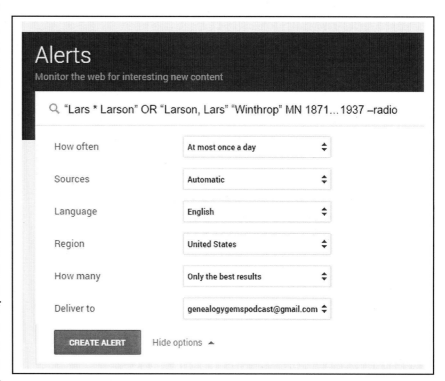

- News
- Blogs
- Web

- Video
- Groups

For example, you may want to follow a story about the possible closing of a library in your area in the news. In that case you would select News as the type of results that you want.

Unless you have unlimited time on your hands, I would recommend selecting "Only the Best Results" in the "How Many" section.

Your final option is to choose where you would like your Google Alert delivered. You can have your alerts sent to any email address.

When you're done, click the Create Alert button. You will automatically be taken to your Manage Your Alerts console.

This is where you will find and edit all of the alerts you have created. The alerts are listed alphabetically. Currently, you can have up to 1000 alerts.

A Word about the "Feed" Delivery Option
In the past you could have your alerts sent to Google Reader via RSS feed, but sadly Google Reader was discontinued July 1, 2013. At that time, the Google Alerts "Feed" option was removed. However, recently Google quietly reinstated it.

If you are an existing feed reader user, please note that currently you can read your feed results in Google Alerts, but not in other readers. Of course this, like many things in the tech world, may change in the future.

Are you new to feeds? A feed allows you to view all results on one page on the web, rather than receiving them through email. Typically a feed address can be copied and pasted into a feed reader so that new alerts will be displayed automatically as they occur. As of this writing though, the feed function does not appear to work that way. If you select the feed option and click the RSS icon on the alert in your dashboard, it takes you to the source code for the feed. Unfortunately, copying the URL (which is the feed address) and pasting it into a web reader such as Feedly at http://www.feedly.com results in an error message.

If you click the actual search query in your dashboard for an alert that you have selected RSS Feed for, the results appear lower on the dashboard page.

So for now, you will likely want to opt for email delivery. However, if you are an avid blog reader user, keep an eye on the feed function in Google Alerts. Hopefully, Google will convert the feed to a standard format that can be read by all feed readers.

Editing Google Alerts

Over time you may find that you are not receiving as many alerts as you expected, or the results are not hitting the nail on the head. In such cases you will want to change the search terms. All editing of alerts is done in the Google Alerts dashboard.

How to Edit a Google Alert:
1. Go to http://www.google.com/alerts and sign in to your account
2. Locate the alert you want to edit in the alphabetical list and click the *Edit* icon that looks like a pencil. (*Image below*)

"L. J. Larson" OR "Larson, L. J." Winthrop MN

"Lars Larson" OR "L. J. Larson" OR "Lars J...

3. Make the desired changes in the edit window.
4. When you're done, click the Update Alert button.

Alerts That Will Further Your Research
Now that you know how to create and manage your alerts, let's discuss what types of alerts might benefit your genealogy research.

Any search that you might conduct for your research is a candidate for a Google alert. However, there are additional sources for alerts to consider as part of your research strategy.

Do you have an ancestor's journal? Consider transcribing it or making a photocopy of it. With your highlighter pen go through and highlight names, places, business names, occupations, addresses, schools attended, churches attended, etc. These are all keywords worthy of searches and Google Alerts.

How about setting up a Google Alert for each surname you are researching in a particular area? Here are a few examples from my own Google Alerts and research:

"Cooke" "Huntingdonshire" 1750..1900
"Cooke" "Brampton" England genealogy
"Sporan" "Chowchilla" CA

Again, you will need to focus your search a bit more for common surnames. Keep it simpler for more rare surnames that won't generate as many results. Refer back to the search strategies from the previous chapters.

How about the neighbors? Pull out the census or the City Directory (*Image right*) for your ancestors' home and set up a few targeted Google alerts that might give you more information about your ancestor's community and the people they were closest to.

The options are only limited by the 1000 alert limit that Google applies.

For a visual overview of setting up Google Alerts watch…
VIDEO: *Google Alerts by the Arlington Heights Memorial Library*
http://www.youtube.com/watch?v=Tzby81W92w4

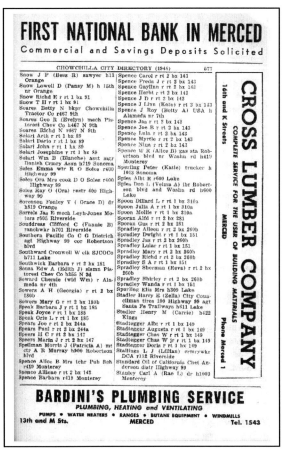

www.GenealogyGems.com

CHAPTER 8
Gmail

URL: http://www.google.com/mail

Not Just Another Email Service

Though millions of people use Gmail, only a small fraction are using it to its full capacity. For the genealogist, those unused capabilities can make the difference between being efficient and getting lost in a mountain of email.

If you already have a free Google account, you can use that same account to create a Gmail account. Even though you may already have another email provider, consider setting up a Gmail account and take it for a test drive. The account is free and doesn't require anything more than a user name and password.

To set up a free Gmail account go to http://www.google.com/mail.

Archiving

Chances are you get a lot of email, and if it's related to your family history research, you probably want to save it for later reference. In many email systems emails are saved to folders, which have some inherent problems:

- You can only save the email to one topic folder.
- The folder may become so full that you lose track of individual emails.
- The subject of the folder may evolve over time and in order to break out a segment of emails on a secondary subject you would have to go through each email and save it to a new folder.

And the list goes on...

With Gmail, folders are a thing of the past. Gmail emails are archived using a tagging system called "labels", similar to how you might tag a multitude of subjects for a blog post, photograph, or a note in Evernote. Once labeled, you can retrieve your email in the future by clicking the label in the left hand column. When there are a large number of emails, thin the results by using the Gmail search engine. Let's look at an example of an email you might receive. (*Image next page*)

There is only one family story that I ever heard growing up. That was the immigration story of my Great-Grandpa Norman Jacobson, from Steigen, Norway. When Norman's father (a fisherman) died of pneumonia around 1905, Norman's mother could not find enough work to support a family, so they immigrated in 1906. His mother, Charlotte, or "Lottie" as she was referred to, brought her 5 children to Minnesota and settled in Cottonwood County.

When I first heard of the Ellis Island site, I excitedly searched the database only to get messages like, "too many to list." Several months later I was searching USGenWeb's site looking for Minnesota indexes where I came across the Iron Mountain Range Genealogy Website. A search on their index brought up both Charlotte and Norman. They both appeared in the 1918 Alien Registration Index of Minnesota, and had also filed Naturalization papers in Minnesota. Of course, I was ecstatic. When the records arrived, they confirmed the family did arrive in 1906. Armed with this new proof, I headed back to Ellis Island.

This email refers to several topics of interest:
- A family surname
- A county where you do a significant amount of research
- Ellis Island

Rather than having to try to decide on just one folder, Gmail allows you to label the email with as many labels as you want.

How to Add a Label to an Email:
1. Open the email in Gmail or click the box to select it from your Inbox list.
2. Click the LABELS button above the email.

3. Select a label you have already created from the drop down list, or select CREATE NEW.
4. If creating a new label, a New Label box will pop up. Type the label name and click

the Create button.

5. You can nest labels by clicking the Nest Label Under box and selecting the label from the drop down menu. *(Image right)*

As you add labels, they appear alphabetically in the column on the left. If you have several they may not all show up. Instead you will see the ones you use most often and then a link to the number of additional labels called More. Just click that link and all the labels become visible. *(Image left)*

You may also find that gadgets like Google Calendar attempt to pop up at the bottom of the labels list. Simply click the three dots icon to minimize Gadgets and provide the maximum amount of room for viewing labels. *(Image right)*

Once you have labeled the email simply click the Archive button at the top of the email and Gmail will tuck it away out of sight. *(Image below)*

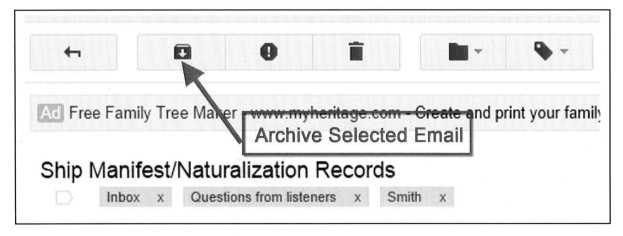

To retrieve the email, click one of the labels on the left that you tagged it with and it will appear in a results list containing all of the emails with that label.

Notice the words now appearing in the Gmail search box *(Image top right)*

label:smith

Gmail is indicating that the emails listed are all labeled as *Smith. Label:* is a Gmail search operator. This means that you can locate emails tagged with any label straight from the Gmail search box. Type *Label:* and then add the label keyword. Make sure there is no space between them.

Working with Labels
As you work with Gmail, chances are you will want to add, edit, and remove labels. There are several ways to do this.

Option 1) Settings:
Click Manage Labels at the bottom of the list of labels in the column on the left. (If Manage Labels doesn't appear, click the More link, which will reveal all of your labels, as well as the Manage Labels link.) *(Image middle right)* This will take you to the Settings dashboard. You can also get there by clicking the Settings icon that looks like a gear in the upper right corner, select Settings, and then select Labels. *(Image bottom right)*

Under the Labels tab you will find settings where you can select which labels are:
- Shown in the left column.
- Hidden so they don't appear in the left column.
- Removed.

Option 2) Inbox:
Edit labels right from your inbox by clicking the down arrow next to the label you want to edit. *(Image next page)*

In addition to hiding and deleting the label, you can:

- Rename the label
- Add a custom color to the label

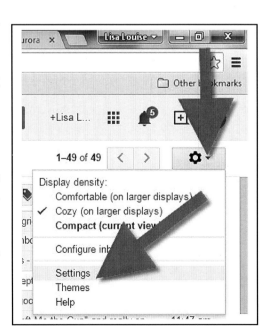

www.GenealogyGems.com

Color-coding your labels can help you stay organized as your list of labels grows. Consider coloring prominent surnames you are researching, or simply using one color for all genealogy-related labels. Customize as you go to suit your needs and make it easier to spot the label you want.

You can also create sublabels (the last option in the list) which is also known as nesting. An example you might create a label called *Genealogy Society* with the sub labels *Programs*, *Projects*, and *Research*.

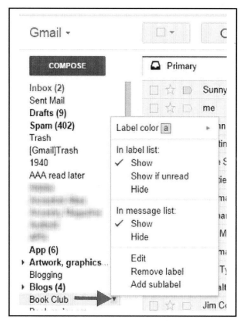

The Power of Search

The really unique feature of Gmail is the dedicated search box. Frequent Google users may assume this is a Google search box. While you can use it to search the internet, it is here primarily to search your Gmail.

Click the down arrow in the box and an advanced search form drops down to guide you through the search process. (*Image right*)

Why is this Gmail search box so important? It applies the power of Google search to your emails! You may never lose track of another email message again...ever!

Let's say that you just found a key research document and you realize that it ties in with a genealogical theory that a distant cousin wrote you about months ago. You want to retrieve the email and review it with the new information. But you have had hundreds of emails from that cousin and can't remember when you received it. No problem! Simply type in the Gmail search box a keyword or two about the topic of the email, (*Image below*)

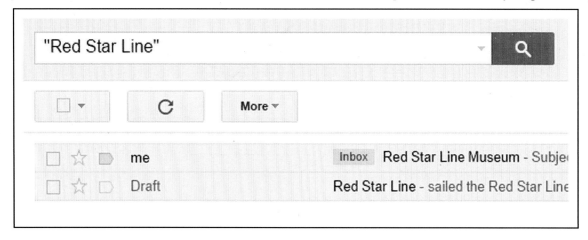

click the Search button, and Gmail will retrieve it for you.

In this example, the topic of the email was about the Red Star Line steamships, and Gmail instantly pulled up two emails that contain that keyword phrase.

Did you notice that I put quotation marks around the phrase to tell Google I only wanted emails that contained that exact phrase? You can also incorporate all of the search techniques and operators used in regular searches including:

- Quotations marks to specify an exact word or phrase.
- Minus sign to eliminate unwanted words.
- Asterisk between two keywords indicating the words may be separated by one or more words. (i.e. *President * Lincoln*)

The Gmail search box is the fastest way to retrieve an archived email. However, if you wish to browse emails that have a particular label, click on the label in the column on the left and all archived emails with that label will appear. And once again, the label also appears in the search box. Google does this in case you would like to search within that set of labeled results. This comes in very handy when you have a large number or emails tagged with a certain label.

To search within labeled results, type additional keywords (and operators if needed) following the label text in the box and click the search button.

This search method makes it possible to pull up potentially hundreds of archived emails with a label and with lightning speed narrow it down to just a specific few! (*Image below*)

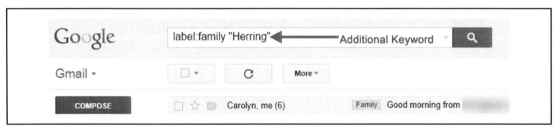

At any time while in your Gmail account, Google search is just a click away. Type your search query into the box and click Search the Web. (*Image below*)

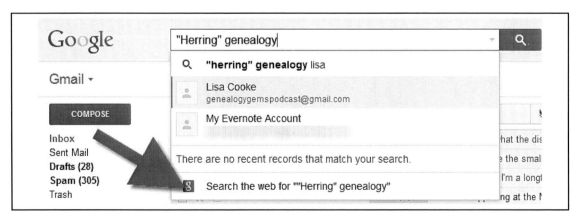

Conversation Threads

When it comes to genealogy, understanding the context of information is critical. And in the case of genealogy-related emails, it is not uncommon to have multiple emails back and forth on a subject. Gmail makes these online conversations very easy to follow with conversation threads. These are much like the threads you find on genealogy message boards.

Rather than wading through all your email trying to follow a conversation, Gmail replies to replies (and so on). They are all displayed in the order received, all in one place, making it easier to understand the context of the messages, and creating a true conversation.

When you open an email message in a conversation, all of your related messages will be stacked on top of each other in order. (*Image right*) This is called Conversation View. To see all the messages included in

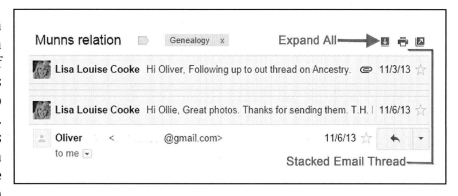

the conversation click the Expand All icon. This is called Expanded View. (*Image below*)

To collapse the thread, click the Collapse All icon (which was previously Expand All.)

Be aware that if you change the subject line, or if the conversation exceeds 100 messages, the conversation will break off into a new thread.

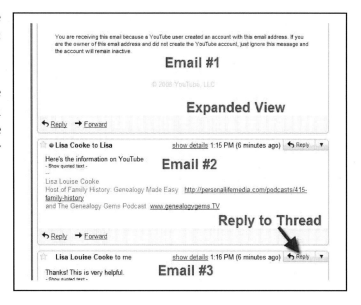

Working Offline

Though you must sign in to your Google account online to gain access, one of the convenient features Gmail offers is the ability to work offline. It is inevitable that at some point the Internet will temporarily go down or you will find yourself on a plane or other location where an Internet connection is unavailable. With the offline app for the Chrome web browser those down times become an opportunity to catch up on your backlog of email.

How to Enable Gmail Offline:

1. From your Chrome browser go to Gmail at mail.google.com and sign in with your Google account.
2. In Gmail click the Setting icon.
3. Click Settings.
4. Click Offline tab.

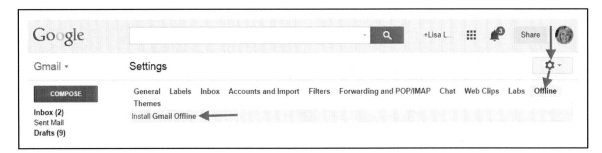

5. Click "Install Gmail Offline" link which will open a new tab in Chrome. (*Image below*)
6. On the Gmail Offline page click the "+ Free" button to install (this button has changed names over time!)
7. In the pop-up window click the Add button.
8. You will then be taken to a refreshed version of the Chrome apps page that will now include Gmail Offline. Click the icon to launch.
9. On the next page you will be prompted to Allow Offline Mail on the computer you are using. Click the button and click Continue. (*Image below*)

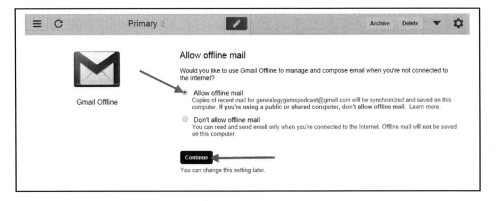

Gmail will download a local cache of your mail, which synchronizes with Gmail's servers any time you're connected. When you lose connectivity, Gmail automatically switches to offline mode so you can keep working. You can even continue to compose email replies because they will be automatically sent the next time Gmail detects a connection.

For information on *troubleshooting* or *uninstalling Gmail offline* – just Google it!

www.GenealogyGems.com

Spam Filter

No matter how good an email client system is, there will always be spam, that unwanted email, often from shady characters. The good news is that Gmail has an excellent spam system built around the same premise as their search engine, which means it's good at discerning content. Gmail has a great track record for accurately labeling and archiving spam email so that you never have to be bothered with it in your inbox. For the occasional messages that do slip through Gmail's filter, it's easy to report the spam and get rid of it. The more spam you mark, the better Google will get at weeding out those annoying messages.

How to Remove Spam from Your Inbox:
1. Click the checkbox next to each unwanted Spam email message.
2. Click the Report Spam button at the top of the email box.

How to Remove Spam Forever:
1. On the left side of the Gmail page click the Spam label.
2. Select the messages you want to delete and click Delete Forever.
3. If you or Google accidentally marks a legitimate message as spam, click

Not Spam at the top of the message. If you just marked it as spam, you can also click Undo immediately after to recover the message.

QUICK TIPS:
#1: Protect desirable email
To help avoid having a wanted email go to the spam folder, add the sender's email address to your Contact list.

#2: Hidden SPAM label
If you don't see the SPAM label in the column on the left, it is "hidden." Unhide it by clicking the Settings icon in the upper right corner of Gmail, click Labels, and locate the Spam label in the list. Click Show and the Spam label will appear in your labels list.

See It in Action!
VIDEO: *5 Ways Gmail Makes Life Easier: Spam Protection*
http://youtu.be/LhlrsJ-PaQw

Fun with Themes

Adding a theme to your Gmail may not help you get through your emails any faster, but it might just make the job a little more pleasant.

How to Add a Theme to Gmail:

1. Click the Settings icon in the upper right hand corner of Gmail.
2. Click on the theme of your choice or select Choose Your Own Colors.
3. The new theme will be instantly applied to your Gmail account.

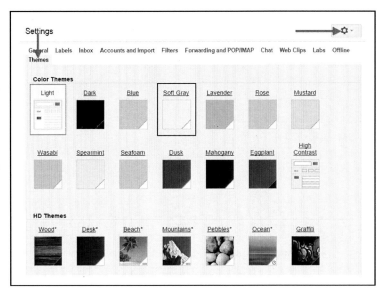

At this point in the book, are you feeling a bit more like a Genealogy Google Ninja? Express yourself with Gmail's Ninja theme!

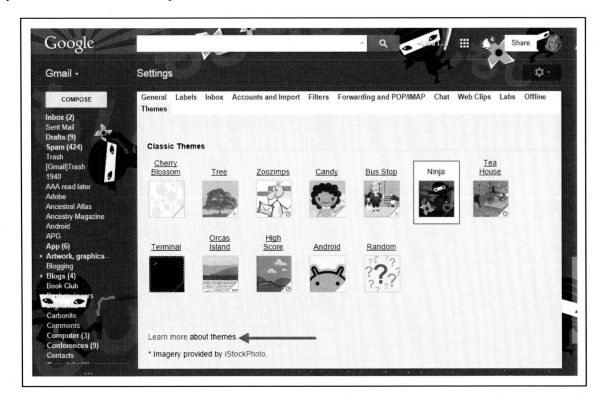

VIDEO: *5 Ways Gmail Makes Life Easier: Themes*
http://youtu.be/ucDePBBlNSM

CHAPTER 9
Google Books

URL: http://books.google.com

Imagine having access to millions of hard-to-find and out of print books for free. That's what you get when you use Google Books! This robust tool lends itself particularly well to genealogy research because old, out-of-copyright books are its specialty. And the good news is that all of the search techniques you learned in the earlier chapters of this book can be used with Google Books.

As you can see below, Google Books has a new look and now includes a portal to Google Play, Google's digital book store on the right side. We will be focusing on the search field on the left side. (*Image below*)

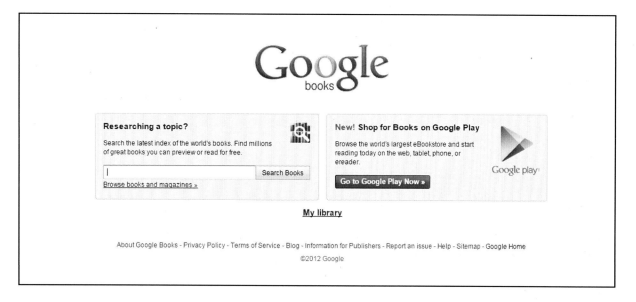

Overview of Google Books
The origin of Google Books goes all the way back to 1996, before Google had become a household word. Graduate computer science students and future Google co-founders Sergey Brin and Larry Page had a shared goal to create digital libraries. They envisioned a future in which vast collections of books would be digitized and "web crawlers" would be used to index the books' content. Computers would be able to analyze the connections between the books, determining their relevance and usefulness by tracking the number and quality of citations from other books.

They eventually developed a web crawler technology that evolved into the PageRank algorithm behind today's Google search. By 2002 a secret "books" project began, which retained the same focus: to digitize all of the books in the world and make them available online.

By 2004 the project was announced as "Google Print" and publishers began partnering with the project. The following year the project's name was changed from Google Print to

Google Books. So you could say that Google's roots can be traced back to books. And Google Books has moved to the forefront as a powerful tool for those tracing their roots.

Book Search works just like Google's web search and delivers the same type of results. Like many of the Google tools, there are advanced search features that can help you achieve even greater results.

Types of Book Content
While browsing and searching Google Books you will come across four different types of content:

- Public Domain Books – full text and downloadable as PDF file
- Out-of-Copyright Books – preview and some full text
- In Copyright, with Publisher's Permission Books – preview and some full text
- Magazines

The books and magazines found on Google Books come from two key sources:

- *The Library Project,* which includes partnerships with several major libraries
- *The Partner Program,* which identifies books through agreements with publishers and authors

Learn more about the Library project from Librarians themselves:
VIDEO: *Google Book Search: UC Library Partnership*
http://www.youtube.com/watch?v=xN0iyzpiZPg

Google takes a partnership approach to acquiring their content, striking agreements to digitize materials under agreed-upon guidelines. However, there has been some controversy over the years as to how books are identified for digitization, how copyright law applies, and what role the actual author plays. Google sought feedback from its users and now works to come to agreements with the various parties and organizations involved. Google Books continues to grow and change. Only time will tell if the goal of digitizing the world's books will be achieved.

You can learn more about how Google Books works and the recent settlement agreement between Google and a broad class of authors and publishers by watching the following video. Please note that this agreement resolves a United States lawsuit, and therefore directly affects only those users who access Book Search in the U.S. The following video begins with a review of the various "views" of books, and then around the 3 minute mark discusses the settlement agreement.

VIDEO: *Google Books Settlement Agreement with Authors and Publishers*
http://youtu.be/J16juV1acCI

Accessing Content

Each book features a "Book Overview" page, including information such as:

- Title
- Author
- Summary paragraph
- Date of publication
- Book length
- Where to Buy and Borrow links

Some books may also have:

- Reviews
- Related books list
- Common terms and phrases
- Scholarly and webpage references
- A map showing places mentioned in the book
- Popular passages from the book
- Table of contents or chapter titles
- Other editions
- ISBN number

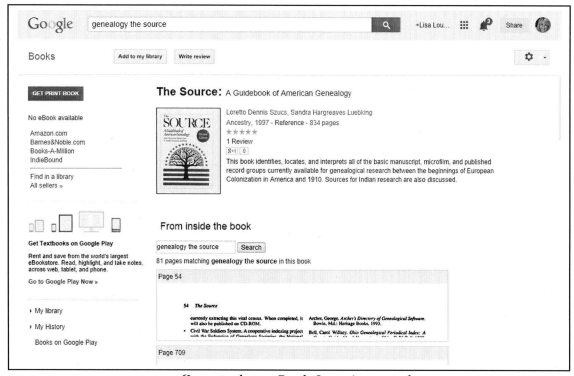

(Image above: Book Overview page)

The Book Overview continues to be expanded as agreements are reached and data is collected by Google. You'll notice that the bulk of modern books now offer 'Previews' thanks to these agreements. It's a great marketing strategy for publishers, so everyone wins. You'll also notice that many books can now be downloaded or purchased right from the Book Overview.

There are four different types of views available in Google Books Search:

View: **Full**
Includes: Out of copyright books or agreement reached with the publisher or author
Pages: All pages are viewable
Download: Yes as PDF if in the Public Domain

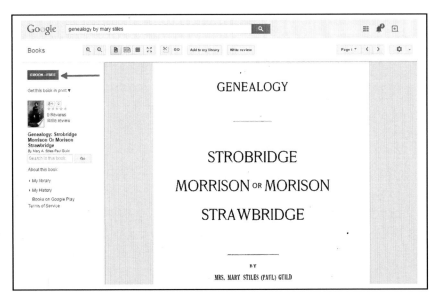

(Image above: Full View)

View: **Preview**
Includes: Books where an agreement has been reached with the publisher or author
Pages: Some pages are viewable
Download: No

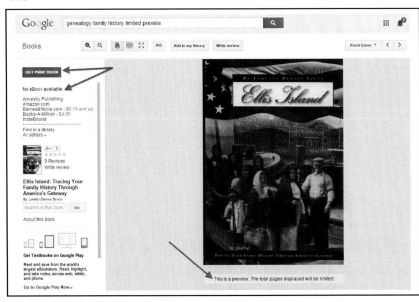

(Image above: Preview)

View:	**Snippet**
Includes:	Some of the remaining books not covered by full view or preview
Pages:	No pages are viewable. Only a very small amount of text showing your search terms (a "snippet") in context is provided.
Download:	No

(Image above: Snippet View)

View:	**No Preview Available**
Includes:	All other remaining books
Pages:	No pages are viewable. Related books will be displayed.
Download:	No

(Image above: No Preview)

A Sample Search

As you can imagine, there is a wealth of genealogical and historical information in the hundreds of thousands of volumes listed in Google Books. Let's do a sample search to explore the methods of locating and using these materials.

While you don't need to be signed in to your Google account in order to do a search, doing so will ensure that you have full usage of all the available features of Google Books. From the Google Books home page at http://books.google.com click the Sign In button in the upper right corner. This will take you to your Google accounts page where you will enter your email address and password, and then click the Sign-In button.

Now you are signed in and back on the Google Books home page ready to search. The first step is to define our search parameters:

Example:
Surnames: Paulus, Chenoweth, and Burket
Where: Randolph County, Indiana
Timeframe: 19th century

Because old county histories are usually out of copyright and in the public domain we have a very good chance of locating the right volume and having full view access to it. We start by typing our search terms *Randolph County Indiana History* into the search box, and clicking the Book Search button. (*Image below*)

There are two key items to notice on the results page and they appear across the top.

Notice first that the Google results are drawing from Books (Note: While working in Google Books, keep in mind that when the term "Book" is used it typically includes all content including magazines.)

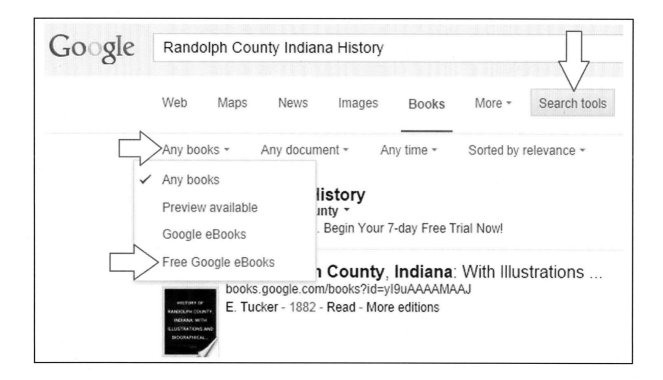

Very often your results list will be quite long and you may elect to start by viewing books that offer the free Full View or Preview. To do that, click the Search Tools button, Select Any Books, and click Free Google eBooks.

If you ever need help with conducting a Google book search, Advanced Search is the ideal place to go.

Google Books Advanced Search

URL: http://www.google.com/advanced_book_search

In the past you could conduct an advanced book search by simply clicking the Advanced Search link just to the right of the Search Books button on the Google Books home page. Unfortunately, the Advanced Search link is nowhere to be found on the home page. However, as quickly as things move in Google's world, it could easily reappear after this new edition of the book is published.

To access Advanced Search you have a few options:
- Go directly to http://www.google.com/advanced_book_search. You can use this URL to access Advanced Book Search regardless of where the link appears (or does not appear) on any given day.
- From the Google Books homepage click the My Library link and you'll find a link to Advanced Search under Settings (the gear icon).
- Conduct a book search and select a book. Once you are on the individual book page, Advanced Book Search can be found again under Settings.

The nice thing about Advanced Search is that it provides easy-to-fill-in boxes when search operators aren't coming to mind. It also prompts you for a variety of other search parameters to choose from that can further assist you in zeroing in on the books you want. (*Image below*)

To narrow our sample search down there are a couple of selections we can make. In the "with at least one of the words" field we can enter our surnames: *Burket Chenoweth Paulus.* This is like telling Google Books to return results for our original search terms and at least one of those surnames.

We can also select the Books Only button. Then in the Publication Date fields we can select "Return content published between" and enter the years *1800* and *1900*. (*Image right: the results of our advanced search*)

Now we are down to just over 438 books. (You can find the number of items in your results list by clicking the Search Tools button again, which will lift the search parameters out of the way revealing the number of results.) A quick glance of the results reveals that the word *county* may be throwing our results off just a bit, particularly since *Randolph* can be a person's name as well. By adding quotation marks around *"Randolph County"* in the search field and rerunning the search we should get even better results.

This next search delivers a manageable number of books to be reviewed. *The History of Wayne County, Indiana* looks promising as it mentions folks from Randolph County as well as one of our specified surnames in the preview. This is an example of the power of the Book Search. If you were searching in a traditional library, you would naturally be pulling books off the shelf with "Randolph County" in their title. However, Google Books reveals that people with the surnames we are looking for who hailed from Randolph County also appear in neighboring county history books!

Click on the title to access the book.

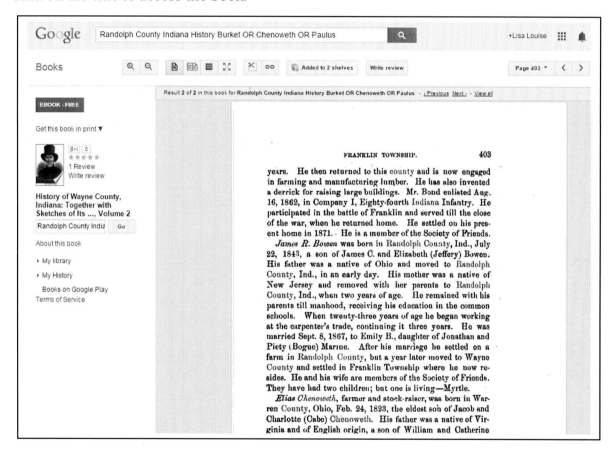

The page viewer (*image above*) offers many familiar options for interacting with the digitized pages of this book. Across the top you will see icons for:

- Zoom
- One and two page views
- Thumbnail view
- Full Screen
- Web clipping
- URL link
- Whether you already have it saved to My Books
- Write Review
- Page number with table of contents drop down menu

- Left and right page scroll buttons

In addition you will also find the following tools for utilizing the images:

Plain Text Converter: This tool has been moved under Settings (the gear icon) and will convert the digitized page to plain typed text. This gives you the flexibility to highlight, copy, and paste portions of the text. Here's an example of text that I was able to copy and paste from the plain text view:

> *"The town now has three stores—one, a general store, kept by Nathan Grave; two groceries, by Wm. Robinson and*

The town now has three stores—one, a general store, kept by Nathan Grave; two groceries, by Wm. Robinson and Hiram Surplice. The practicing physicians are: Drs. Wm. Williams, James Courtney and W. T. Griffiths. Blacksmiths: Thomas White, Hiram Gist, A. Jackson. Chairmaker, Charles Wolverton. The town has two churches, Methodist and Disciples, and lodges of Odd Fellows and Masons.

> *Hiram Surplice. The practicing physicians are: Drs. Wm. Williams, James Courtney and W. T. Griffiths. Blacksmiths: Thomas White, Hiram Gist, A. Jackson. Chairmaker, Charles Wolverton. The town has two churches, Methodist and Disciples, and lodges of Odd Fellows and Masons."*

While in Plain Text view you have the ability to download the plain text version of the book as a PDF or EPUB document to your computer. To return to the digitized page click the Page Images link in the upper right corner.

Clip Tool: This tool gives you incredible flexibility for using and sharing portions of the book. Simply click the Clip Tool icon and your cursor will become a plus sign. Place the plus cursor in the upper left corner of the section you want to clip and click and drag the cursor to create a box around the text. A clip window will then automatically pop up giving you the following options:

> **Selection Text** – This can be highlighted, copied, and pasted in other documents. By clicking the Translate link, it can also be translated into other languages. *Application Example:* You are researching your German ancestors and have located a book written in German. You can select portions and automatically translate them.

> **Image** – The clipped text now resides on Google's servers, and the image of the clip can be linked to with the URL provided in the clip box.

> **Embed** – If you have a website or family history blog you can quickly and easily share your findings online. The clip tool automatically generates the HTML code you will need to include your clipped text on your webpages. Just highlight, copy, and paste the code.

Link Tool: This tool provides you with a unique URL for the book that you can copy and paste into an email or instant message. The link will take the recipient directly to the book and the page that you are currently working with. *Application Example:* Another researcher across the country is collaborating with you. You can instantly send your newest discovery to them.

Download PDF Tool: Save a PDF version of the book to your computer hard drive for reading and reference. Go to Settings > Download PDF.

Search Within the Book

To search further within this book just type keywords into the search box in the column on the left side of the page and click the Go button. For example, you can enter an additional surname you are interested in. In this example (*image below*), searching on the name *Lightner* instantly reveals one occurrence of the name on page 498.

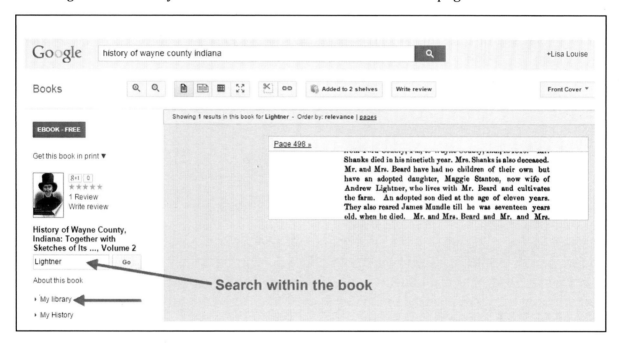

You can use the search operators we discussed earlier when you are searching within any book in Google Books.

My Library

Another powerful tool within Google Books is My Library. It allows you to create a virtual library within Google Books of the books you have found. To get to My Library just click the My Library link. (*Image above*)

Here you can:
- Create a My Library profile.
- Import books from your searches into My Library for future reference.
- Export My Library as an XML document.
- Organize your books on "shelves" by topic.
- Rate each book with a 5 star rating system.
- Add notes to each book. Notes on public books will be public, and notes on private books will be private.

- Add labels to each book. *Application Example:* Surnames, locations, and other genealogical topics of interest.
- Write a review of the book for the benefit of all researchers.

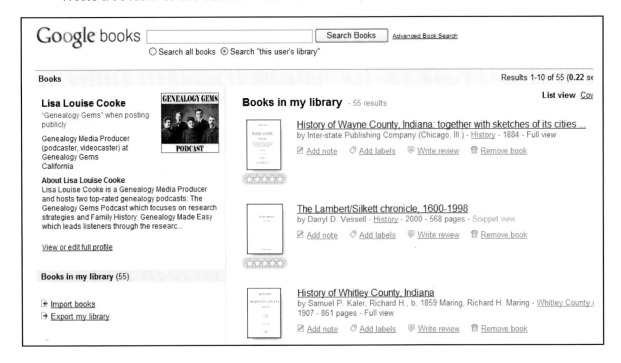

(Image Above: Example of My Library)

Shelves

As your Google Books My Library grows you'll want to stay organized, and shelves are a great way to do it. You can add customized "shelves" to keep track of different kinds of books (like genealogy how-tos, or books related to a certain family.) Create as many as you want and mark them private or public as desired.

How to Setup a New Shelf in My Library:

1. Click the red New Shelf button.
2. Type in a name for your shelf and a description of the types of books you will be including.
3. Select whether you want the shelf to be public or private. Any notes included on books on public shelves will be visible to everyone. You can change the setting in the future by clicking on the shelf and then going to Settings > Edit Properties.
4. Click the My Library link from any page and you will see your shelves displayed. First in the list will be default shelves such as My Books on Google Play, Purchased, Reviewed, Recently Viewed (very handy finding a book you looked at recently), and Browsing History. Your custom shelves will be listed alphabetically. The privacy setting can be adjusted for each of these as well.

How to Add a Book to a Shelf in My Library:

1. Pull up the book in Google Books.

www.GenealogyGems.com

2. From the book page, hover your mouse over the Add to My Library button and click on the desired shelf from the drop down list.

(Image above: Shelves in My Library)

Notes

With notes you can add even more customized information about the books in your My Library. Notes are a way to track specific information about a book. For example, you may want to list surnames you research that apply to the book, or a particular page of interest for future reference. (*Image below*)

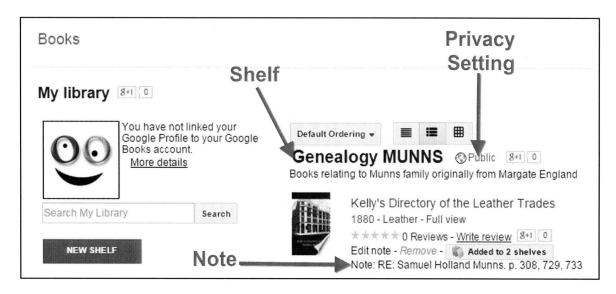

But first, it's important to understand what will and won't be displayed publicly. Google explains it this way: "When you add reviews, ratings, notes, or labels to a book - or when you add a book to a public bookshelf in your My Library page - that information will be publicly displayed on Google Books. A book you add to a My Library bookshelf that you marked private will not be publicly displayed (although the reviews and ratings added to that book will still be publicly displayed)."

Unfortunately the statement above doesn't specify that Notes are still public even when your book is on a Private shelf. But they do say that Reviews and Ratings are still public. This creates a bit of confusion. In my own testing, notes that I made on books on private shelves did not appear publicly on the book listing. And because the shelves are private, they don't show publicly in search results. Bottom line: privacy for notes is not spelled out by Google for books on private shelves, and that means it is best not to consider privacy guaranteed. Don't post anything you wouldn't want others to see, even though my best determination is that they won't see your notes if they are on books that reside on private shelves.

How to Add a Note to a Book:
1. Go to My Library.
2. From the list of shelves in the left hand column click on a shelf, or alternatively click the More link for the desired shelf. (*Image right*)
3. From List View click Add Note for the book you want.
4. In the pop up box type your note.
5. Click Save.

How to Delete the Personalized Data You Added to a Book:
1. In MyLibrary access the shelf where the book resides
2. From the shelf page you will see your note under the book. Click Edit Note. (*Image below*)
3. Erase the unwanted text.
4. Click Save.

Keys to Success

1. *Be aware that Book Search isn't perfect.* Not every page of text is a high-enough quality scan that Google can read it perfectly.
   Therefore, using the search feature will not always pick up your search terms. In the end it comes down to using your

best judgment. For example, I have viewed the microfilm version of the *History of Randolph County Indiana* by E. Tucker and located family surnames. However, one of those surname did not come up in the Google Books search results for that book. This was because the page containing the surname was a bit distorted when digitized, making it impossible for Google Books search to identify the word using Optical Character Recognition (OCR.). In situations this like, the key to success is to try a variety of searches. For example, if the surname doesn't appear in results, try searching for the first name of the individual, or other names with which they were associated.

1. Take full advantage of the MyLibrary feature and keep records of what you've searched. Book Search is vast so keeping notes as you search will help avoid duplication of effort and ensure you get the most out of your time spent.

2. Utilize the Advanced Search and try your searches from many different angles. Search is not an exact science and takes some trial and error.

3. Learn from fellow genealogists about how they use Google Books.
   VIDEO: ***Google Book Search: Researching Your (Ancestral Roots)***
   http://www.youtube.com/watch?v=UwnbCmVrISQ

CHAPTER 10
Google News Archive

http://news.google.com/newspapers

Newspapers are one of the most interesting and diverse genealogical sources available. That's why it was exciting news when Google acquired paperofrecord.com in June of 2006. It signaled their interest in historic newspapers, in addition to their growing Google News offering which launched in 2002.

Back in 2006 the Google News Archive was simply an index of other webpages containing historic newspapers. In 2008 they took a step in line with the Google Books project by digitizing newspapers to add to the archive. And one of my all-time favorite Google tools came online in the now defunct Google Labs. It was called the Google News Timeline, and was featured prominently in the first edition of this book.

Sadly, the Timeline was discontinued without fanfare or explanation. I'd like to take a moment to address this because inevitably each time Google changes or discontinues something a fire storm erupts online (This is often the case with Ancestry.com as well!) While it is certainly frustrating as an end-user to have favorite tools come to an end, it's really not that surprising. It helps to remember that in many areas Google is carving out new territory. The internet is much like the Wild West, with few rules and folks figuring out what's possible as they go. Not everything will be sustainable. I would rather take the occasional lumps than not have Google actively innovating.

Google made a valiant attempt to digitize newspapers. But alas, it wasn't proving profitable, and the future of newspapers generally had certainly come in to question. In August 2011 they threw in the towel and quietly merged the archive into Google News at https://news.google.com.

At first glance it looked like they had taken down all of the existing digitized newspapers because there the link to the Google News Archive from the Google News homepage was gone. However, there is a back door entrance and you will find it at http://news.google.com/newspapers. Here you will find a stripped down alphabetical index of all of the existing digitized content. (*Image below*) Even though it isn't fancy, if the

newspaper you need is on the list you are in for a gold mine of information. So before you pull out your credit card for a subscription newspaper website, explore the Google News Archive.

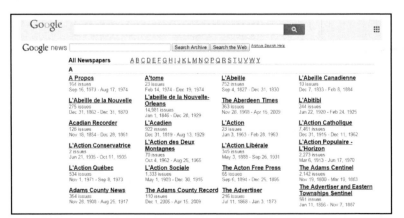

Types of Content

There are a couple of different types of content that you will find in the News Archive.

The first type is ***partner content*** which was digitized by Google through their News Archive Partner Program. Google partnered with publishers and repositories to make their newspaper holdings available as part of the News Archive search. If the content was already digitized and online, Google indexed it and made it available.

If the content had not been digitized, Google then worked with the copyright holder to digitize it and make it full-text searchable online. When you click on a News Archive Partner Program item, you will be taken to a Google-hosted page containing the article within the newspaper page.

The second type of content is ***online archival materials*** that Google has "crawled." You can determine if the article is from another source found by Google by looking at the details listed beneath the search results. And look for the "Get this newspaper" link in the right hand column of the newspaper viewer. (*Image below*)

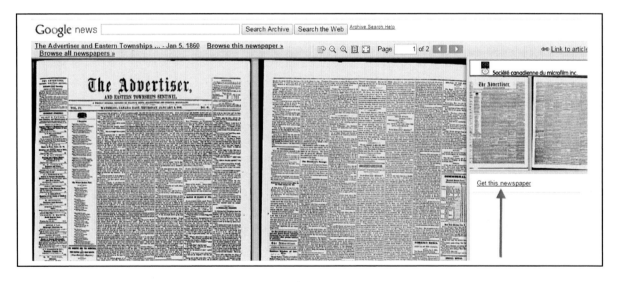

A third type of content that originally appeared in search results was ***pay-per-view***, which required a fee to access. However this content was discontinued when the project was retired.

As I've mentioned before, newsworthy events that occurred in your ancestor's community at the time they lived there are great topics to research and learn more about. For instance, if your ancestor was living in San Francisco during or around the time of the Great Earthquake of 1906 you may want to search the News Archive for related articles. Here are examples of the type of results we've discussed:

Search: *The San Francisco Earthquake 1906*

1. News Archive Partner Content (indexed or digitized)

Result: *The San Francisco Earthquake*, The Sydney Morning Herald, June 19, 1906, Page: 2.

2. Online Archival Materials (crawled and catalogued by Google)
   Result: *Literary Women in the San Francisco Earthquake*, The New York Times, May 12, 1906, Page: BR311.

Searching for Newspaper Content

In addition to the discontinuation of active newspaper digitization, there have also been some changes to how search applies to the Google News Archive. As I mentioned before, the News Archive was technically rolled into Google News, even though there is no link to the archive from the homepage. It's clear that the focus of Google News is current news. Google considers content older than 30 days to be part of News Archive, but archive search is no longer available within Google News. Are you confused yet? My guess is that the reason for this is simple: Google wants you to use Google.com to search for news. Because the Google News Archive index page has very limited search capabilities, here are strategies that you can use to successfully search for historical newspapers.

The Search Box

It's an obvious first choice, but it's important to understand that the search box is essentially an automated site search (refer back to chapter 4 for more on Site Search.) This means that searching for *George Moore* in the News Archive search box (*image below*) is the same as going to Google and running the following search.

"George Moore" site:http://news.google.com/newspapers

You can add any combinations of keywords and phrases and search operators in the search box as you wish, and all of the newspapers will be searched. Which brings us to one of the limitations of the Google News Archive: there is no built in mechanism for searching one particular paper.

Let's look at an example: Go to http://news.google.com/newspapers and click on The Daily News Texan. An easy way to get there quickly would be to click the letter "D" at the top of the page since the entire index is alphabetized.

QUICK TIP: An even faster way to look for a particular newspaper is to use your web browser's Find feature (Control + F). In this case I would search for the word *Texan*.

Notice that even when you are in a specific newspaper, the search box is still only set up to Search Archive or Search the Web. There is no 'search within' type search box as there is with Google Books. (*Image below*)

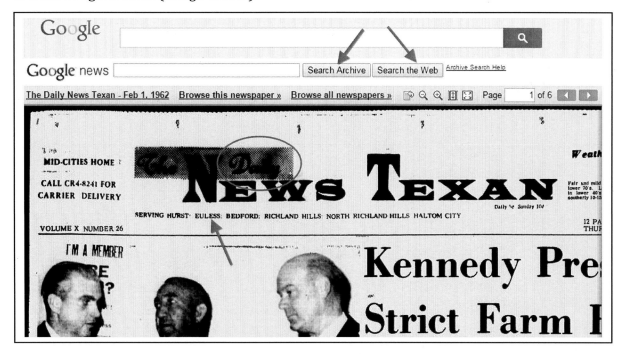

This means you will need to select keywords specific to the particular newspaper as best you can. Notice that the word "Daily" on the front page (*circled in the image above*) is in a somewhat cursive type face, and is not as prominent as "News Texan." That means that chances are the OCR may not pick that word up. However, there are some keywords unique to this paper: the local town it serves such as Hurst and Euless. So if we want Google News to search primarily this newspaper (or at least include it in the search results) we may want to try the following search query:

Euless "George Moore" site:news.google.com/newspapers

Unfortunately, the truth is that due to a variety of factors, this strategy only works sometimes. Give it a try, and then move on to the following strategies.

Try variations of your search
Because OCR isn't 100% accurate, searching for related alternative keywords and phrases may pick up an article you would have otherwise missed. For instance, rather than searching on your grandfather's name, search for your grandmother. After searching for *obituary* try *death notice*.

Browse the Newspaper

There's a good chance that the OCR didn't pick up the keywords you searched in every newspaper in which they appear. If you find a newspaper title in the index, try the old fashioned approach of browsing.

Google News Archive's viewer has many of the same features you have probably found in other online digital content viewers, including:

- Browse this Newspaper (takes you to a page where you can browse by timeframe and date, as well as control the size of the thumbnails pages displayed)
- Zoom in and out
- Page Browsing (click left and right arrows or jump to page numbers)
- Full page navigation thumbnail (click the blue box and move it around the thumbnail to navigate the large page.)
- Link to article (click this link, then click the article you want and Google will assign the article its own unique URL)
- Related Articles list

(Image below: The Google News viewer)

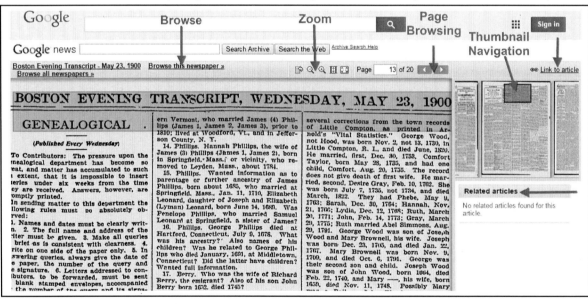

QUICK CLIP TIP: Since the Google News Archive viewer doesn't include a clipping tool, I recommend using the free Evernote program at https://evernote.com. Evernote is the ideal choice because although it will save the image clipped as an image file, it will also apply OCR to the clipping, making it once again keyword searchable! Sign up for a free Evernote account and then download the free Evernote desktop application to your computer. Open the Evernote program, and then pull up the newspaper page you want. Right-click on the Evernote icon in your task bar and select Clip Screenshot from the pop up menu. (*Image next page*) Using your mouse, simply draw a box around the desired section of the newspaper and release. A web clipping image of that portion of the page will be instantly saved to Evernote as a note. If you can't fit the entire newspaper section that you want on the screen at one time, clip it in chunks, and use Evernote's "merge" function to merge them all together into one note.

(Image below: clipping newspaper articles in Evernote)

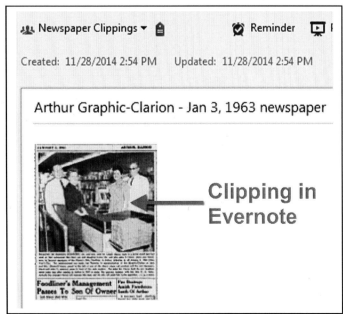

www.GenealogyGems.com

CHAPTER 11
Google Scholar

http://scholar.google.com

If you are interested in focusing on scholarly work on a particular topic or family, Google Scholar is the tool for you. You can restrict your searches to courts, universities, academic publishers, and other scholarly content providers with this powerful free website.

Google Scholar allows you to search all scholarly literature, and explore related works, citations, authors, and publications. It can also help you keep up to date with recent developments in any area of research with the built in link to Google Alerts. And if you have published your own works, Google Scholar can check to see who is citing your publications, graph those citations over time, and compute the citation metrics.

Start by entering your search query in the search box. You will notice under the search box there are some filtering options. These change every so often, but typically you will have the choice between Articles and Case Law. Recently they have dabbled with including an option for including Patents with Articles which is also convenient.

You can also access the advanced search tool for Google Scholar by clicking the down arrow in the search box. (*Image above*)

After you have run your initial search, you will find additional search tools on the left side of the search results page. (*Image right*)

These include my favorite, the custom range search. It operates just like the numrange search operator, restricting your results to webpages that mention specified years.

Google Scholar also features its own My

www.GenealogyGems.com

Library feature, much like Google Books does. You will first need to activate it to make use of it. Click the My Library link at the top of the Google Scholar home page. On the next page, click the Enable button. From that point forward, as you locate articles through your searches, you can save them to your library so that you can read or cite them later. To add an item to your My Library, just click Save below a search result. (*Image below*)

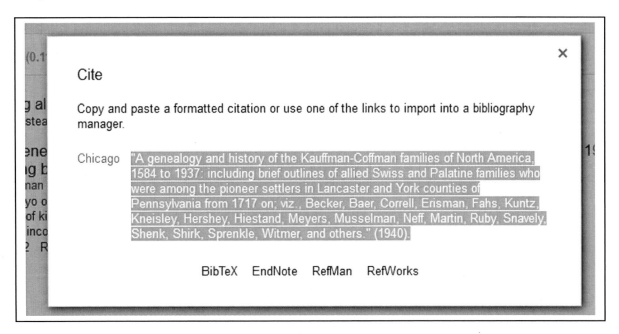

[BOOK] A **genealogy** and history of the Kauffman-Coffman **families** of **North** America, 1584 to 1937: including brief outlines of allied Swiss and Palatine **families** who ...
CF Kauffman - 1940 - books.google.com
... A third is numerous **north** of the city of Berne in the district of Ober Aargau at Hellsau, Herzogenbuchsee, and ... In 1558 a military muster roll was made in the circuit of Steffisburg containing 209 **families**; but it did not contain any Kaufman which would indicate the **family** had ...
Cited by 2   Related articles   Cite   Save   More

Click My library anytime to see all the articles you have saved, and search their full text. If you create a Scholar profile, any articles you have written will automatically be included in your library. You can also import everything you've cited.

To cite a source that you have located in Google Scholar, just click the Cite button under the item on the results page. The Cite box will pop up, and the citation will be highlighted and ready for you to copy by pressing Control + C on your keyboard. We've got to love a Google tool that makes source citation this easy! (*Image below*)

Cite

×

Copy and paste a formatted citation or use one of the links to import into a bibliography manager.

Chicago   "A genealogy and history of the Kauffman-Coffman families of North America, 1584 to 1937: including brief outlines of allied Swiss and Palatine families who were among the pioneer settlers in Lancaster and York counties of Pennsylvania from 1717 on: viz., Becker, Baer, Correll, Erisman, Fahs, Kuntz, Kneisley, Hershey, Hiestand, Meyers, Musselman, Neff, Martin, Ruby, Snavely, Shenk, Shirk, Sprenkle, Witmer, and others." (1940).

BibTeX   EndNote   RefMan   RefWorks

Also conveniently located on Scholar search results pages is the "Create Alert" button. This makes it a breeze to put Google to work for you tracking down newly added articles with just a click.

CHAPTER 12
Google Patents

http://google.com/patents

Launched back in 2006, Google Patents is yet another free tool provided by Google. This search engine indexes patents and patent applications from the United States Patent and Trademark Office (USPTO) as far back as 1790, and the European Patent Office (EPO), and World Intellectual Property Organization (WIPO) back to 1978. The public domain documents, totaling approximately 8 million that can be retrieved from each of these databases include the entire collection of:
- Published patent applications
- Granted patents

Optical character recognition (OCR) has been applied to the pages making them keyword searchable. This searchability includes all US patents and published patent applications. But of course, as is always the case with OCR, the searchability isn't perfect. However, you have all of the Google search strategies that we have covered thus far at your fingertips to improve your chances of a find.

As with most tools, the easiest way to learn how to use it is just to use. So let's see if we can locate the earliest patent application on record by Thomas Edison for the telephone.

How to Search for a Patent:
1. Go to http://google.com/patents.
2. Enter your search terms in the search box, incorporating search operators and other strategies as applicable.
3. Click the Search button.
4. On the search results page, click Search Tools. (*Image below*)
5. From the drop down menus select filters. In this example I will filter by Filing Date.

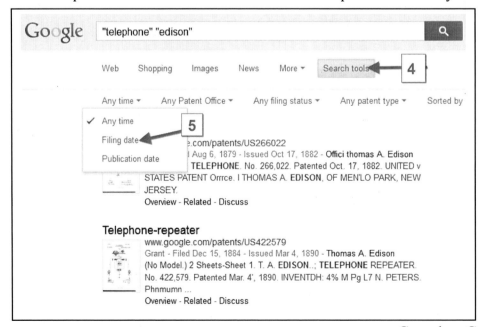

www.GenealogyGems.com

6. In the pop up box enter the specific desired time frame for the search. (*Image right*)
7. Click the Go button.
8. Now the results show the oldest document on file that includes both *telephone* and *Edison* at the top of the list. (*Image below*)
9. Continue to filter your search as desired. For example, if you only want design patents, click on Any Patent Type and select Design from the drop down menu and re-run your search.

It's important to keep in mind that today's terminology may not apply to days gone by. For example, if you are looking for very early automobile-related patents you might be well-served to also include alternative keywords such as *"horseless carriage"*.

When you find a patent of interest click the title to access it. You'll find a good deal of clickable and valuable information here including exportable source citations, the original image, and even a link to all patents by that inventor. (*Image below*)

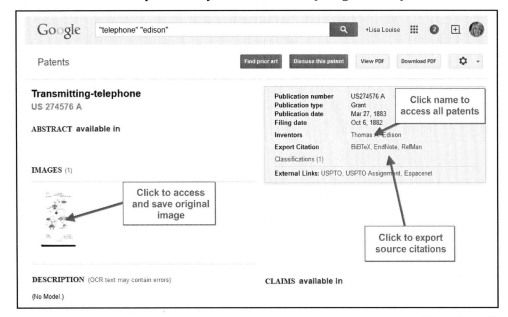

For more help with searching within Google Patents, try the Advanced Patent Search at http://www.google.com/advanced_patent_search. (*Image below*)

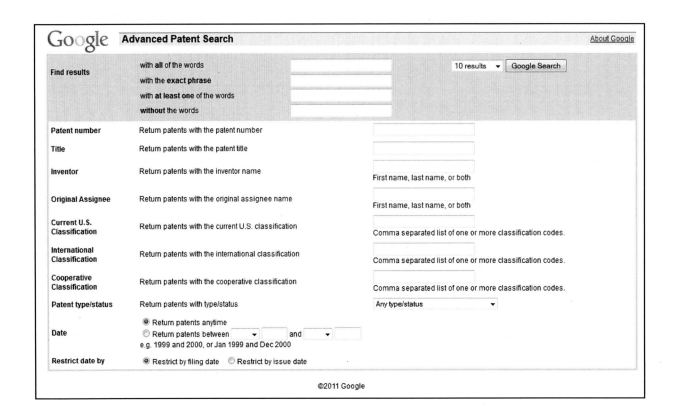

CHAPTER 13
Google Translate

http://translate.google.com

Chances are at some point in your research you will find yourself needing to do some translation, whether it is a website, book, or letter. More than once I've come across a website that mentions an unusual surname that I'm working on but it's in another language. This is where translation websites like Google Translate can really come in handy. Even if they don't do a perfect job of translating they will be able to give you the general idea of what the text says.

Google Translate has come a long way since its debut in 2007. It is not only a website tool... (*image right*)

...but it's also built right into Google.com's search page... (*image below, left*)

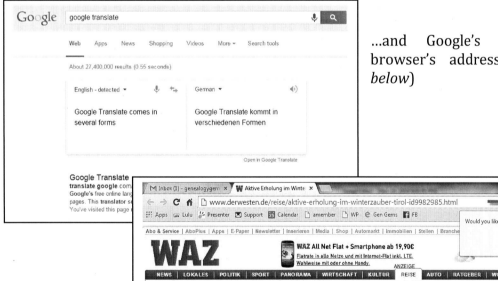

...and Google's Chrome web browser's address bar! (*Image below*)

Here's a quick video that shows you how Google Translate figures out how to translate your items.

See It For Yourself:
VIDEO: *Inside Google Translate*
http://youtu.be/Rq1dow1vTHY

Using Google Translate

As of this writing you have the option to translate:
- Text
- Webpages
- Documents

As you will see below, the Google Translate website has changed a bit. It now sports a cleaner look, as well as some cool new features.

How to Translate Text:
1. Go to http://www.google.com and type in *Google Translate* or go directly to https://translate.google.com.
2. Highlight and copy the text from any webpage or document on your computer. (Control + C on your keyboard will copy the text to your computer's clipboard.)
3. Paste the text into the translation box on the left, or type it in yourself. (Control + V)
4. Select the language of the text entered into the box from the Translate From drop down menu.
5. Select the language you want to translate the text into from the Translate Into drop down menu.
6. The translation will automatically appear.

Here's an example of German text translated with Google Translate. (*Image below*)

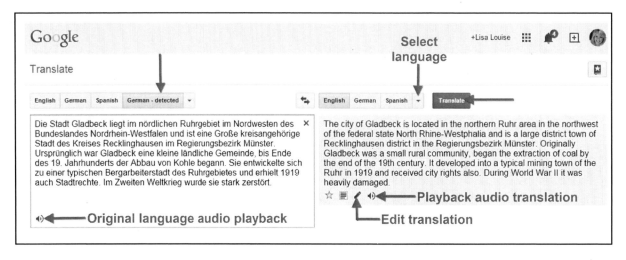

Google Translate automatically detected that the text was in German. This feature can prove very helpful when you're not sure of the language of the text. After copying and pasting the text into the box on the left, you can then click the down arrow above the box on the right to select the desired language, and click the Translate button. The translated text includes an edit button because computerized translation is not perfect and you may want to clean it up a bit.

Another terrific feature is the audio playback. Not only can you playback an audio translation, but you can also click the audio button in the original text box to hear what it sounds like in the original language.

How to Translate a Webpage:
1. Go to the webpage you want to translate.
2. Highlight the webpage URL and copy. (Control + C)
3. Go to http://translate.google.com.
4. Paste (Control + V) the URL into the translation box on the left. (*Image below*)

5. Click English or select the desired language from the drop down menu.
6. Click the Translate button.

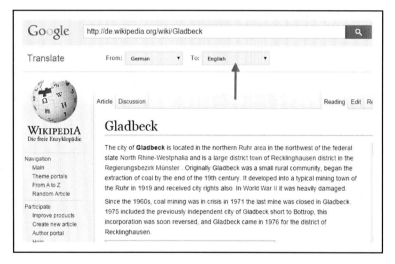

(Image above: translated webpage including Google Translate tool at the top)

How to Translate a Document:
1. Go to http://translate.google.com.
2. Click the Translate a Document link. (*Image right*)
3. Click the Choose File button.
4. In the pop up window locate the document you want to translate on your computer hard drive.

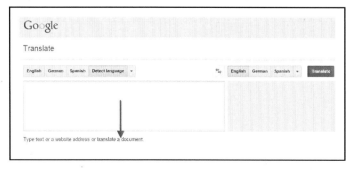

www.GenealogyGems.com

5. Click Open. (*Image below*)

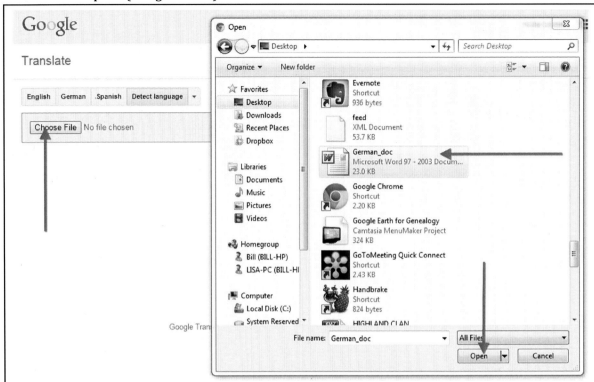

6. Click Detect Language.
7. Click English or select a language from the drop down menu.
8. Click the Translate button.

The translated document will appear on your screen. (*Image right*) You can easily copy the text and paste it into another program such as Word or Evernote.

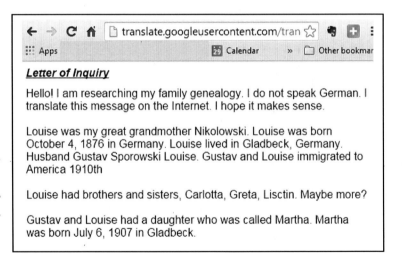

Cross Language Search

A genealogist knows that it is critical to consult maps of the time period being researched because borders often change. Along with border changes come language changes. For example, you may be researching German ancestors and have documents written in German, but you should consult with a Polish or Russian archive for assistance. Cross Language Search allows you to perform searches between any two languages supported by Google Translate. The translation process is the same. Simply select the desired languages from the drop down menus above each text box.

Going Global

Perhaps you have a family history blog or website where you discuss your Italian (or any other ethnicity) ancestors. By incorporating Google Translate into your website or blog, you can make it accessible to researchers and distant cousins who do not speak English. Think how much more far-reaching this will make your website, and how it may facilitate being able to make connections!

By adding the Translate gadget to your webpage, you can offer instant access to automatic translations of that page. Adding the gadget is quick and easy. It will also include all of the new languages recently added.

How to Add Google Translator to Your Webpages:

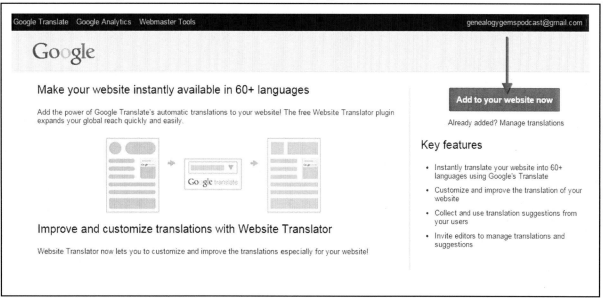

1. Go to the Google Translate Tools and Resources page at http://translate.google.com/translate_tools.
2. Click Add to Your Website Now. (*Image above*)
3. Type in your website address. (*Image right*)
4. Select ENGLISH.
5. Click NEXT.
6. Follow the prompts to customize your translation.
7. Click Get Code.
8. Copy the HTML code automatically generated by Google.
9. Paste the code into your website source code as instructed.
10. The translator will automatically appear on your website.
11. Click Manage Translations for more assistance at https://translate.google.com/manager/website/.

Google Translate Extension for Chrome

If you use Google's Chrome web browser, you can add the free Google Translate extension from the Chrome Web Store at http://chrome.google.com/webstore/category/extensions. Just search for *Google Translate* in the search box. With the extension you can highlight or right-click on a section of text, and then click on the Translate icon that appears next to it to translate it to your desired language. You can even translate an entire web page by clicking the translate icon on the browser toolbar.

Google Translator Toolkit

Google Translator Toolkit (*image below*) is a web application where you can edit the translations that Google Translate automatically generates. It's different from Google Translate because Google Translate provides "automatic translations" produced solely by technology, without human translator intervention. By comparison, Google Translator Toolkit allows actual translators to work faster and more accurately with the aid of technology like Google Translate.

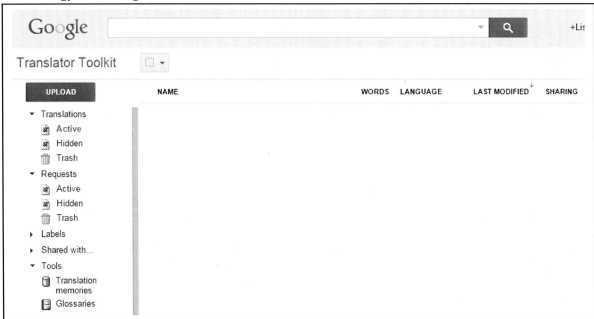

While Google Translator Toolkit may not be something you need right now, it's good to be aware that you can:

- Upload Word documents, OpenOffice, RTF, HTML, text, and Wikipedia articles.
- Use previous human translations and machine translation to "pre-translate" your uploaded documents.
- Use Google's simple editor to improve the pre-translation.
- Invite others (via email) to edit or view your translations.
- Download documents to your desktop in their native formats (i.e. Word, OpenOffice, RTF, or HTML.)
- Publish your Wikipedia translations back to Wikipedia.

To learn more about how the Translator Tool Kit works...
VIDEO: *Translator Tool Kit*
http://www.youtube.com/watch?v=C7W2NJFdoIg

Bye Bye to Google Labs and Google Script Converter

In the first edition of this book we discussed Google Labs, the place where Google test drove new and innovative ideas they were considering adding to their toolkit. It was a fun place to explore and has spawned several excellent web applications. However, Google Labs, which included beta projects like Script Converter, shut its doors in July of 2011.

Also gone is our "just for fun" Pig Latin search! I know, it makes absolutely no difference to genealogy. But genealogists do like to have fun. The closest you'll get to Pig Latin these days is converting the black

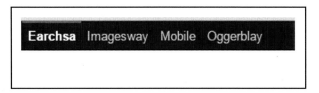

toolbar to it. Head to https://www.google.com/?hl=xx-piglatin&gws_rd=ssl for a change of pace. (*Image right*)

A Few Quick Tricks for Research Trip Planning

If you are fortunate enough to be able to take a trip to the land of your ancestors, or if you need to send an overseas archive payment for services rendered, Google can help you determine the currency type as well as the conversion rate.

Not sure what the currency is used in Romania? Go to Google.com and type in the search box:

1 U.S. Dollar in Romanian Money

(*Image right*) You not only have the answer in the search result, but you also have this handy currency converter where you can enter specific amounts and track trends. Click the Disclaimer link in the bottom right corner for details on use.

Need to know what the weather will be like for your trip to Ellis Island? In the Google search box type:

Weather 07305 (the postal code)

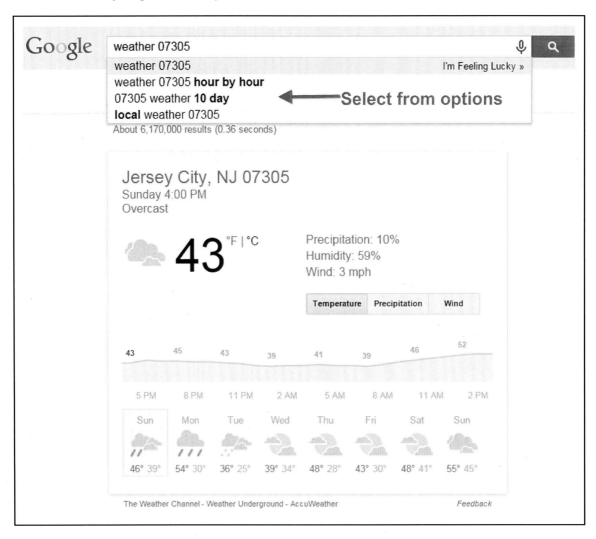

Just a few quick tricks for making your research trip planning a little easier!

CHAPTER 14
YouTube

http://youtube.com

Back in the first edition of this book the title of this chapter was "YouTube and Google Videos." YouTube and Google Video were both founded in 2005 as video sharing websites. By July 2006, YouTube had surged ahead by serving up 100 million videos per day to its users. Shortly thereafter in November, Google purchased YouTube and it remains the world's most popular online video channel. In August 2012, a year after this book's first publication, Google Video (not to be confused with Google Videos which is Google's video search engine) was shut down and the videos were moved to YouTube.

YouTube is best known for its quirky and funny user uploaded videos. But much like iTunes, it's not just for teenagers anymore. Amidst those billions of hours of video hosted on the YouTube website are a number of videos that would be very useful to the genealogist on several levels.

Back in 2011 when this book was first published, a search on the word *genealogy* in YouTube resulted in over 3,400 videos. Today that number is approaching 100,000, and "family history" generates close to the same. (*Image below*) So as you can see, there are a lot of videos to choose from and the number is growing every day.

When browsing and searching YouTube keep your eye out for videos that can help you in your research by providing:
- Original footage of events all the way back to the invention of the movie camera.
- Family History documentaries created by users that may include your family.
- Instructional videos that will help you become a better researcher, create a family heirloom, or learn the latest genealogy software.
- Video tours of archives, libraries, and other repositories that will help you prepare for and get the most out of your visit.
- Interviews with genealogy experts and vendors.
- Entertaining videos that add enjoyment to one of the world's most popular hobbies.
- Your family in other family's home movies.

Yes, you heard me right on that last one. It's not so far-fetched to think that you could find an old home movie on YouTube that happens to include one of your relatives. Uploading old photos is common place now, and it's easier than ever now to transfer old reels of film to digital files. Let me give you an example.

Many of my Genealogy Gems Podcast listeners write in to share their stories of using the techniques I discuss on the show and website to achieve genealogical success. Some of my favorite stories include video. One woman told me that by searching on the name of a small town in South Carolina she found a video of her uncle walking down Main Street in someone else's home movies. Another woman described how she put the idea to the test by searching for a particular parade that her grandmother had participated in back in 1946. Her grandmother was the waving princess on a float that won a major prize. Though the family has the trophy, they don't have any photos of film of the event. Within minutes of searching on the name of the parade and year, she found her grandmother floating by 1 minute and 26 seconds into the first video!

Have I convinced you to give YouTube a try? OK, let's go!

A Word about Video Content

Because YouTube is geared to the entertainment-focused user, you may want to avoid browsing and simply concentrate on using the search box. It is your best tool for finding videos of interest.

Before we go further, let's talk about YouTube content. YouTube does have specific terms of use rules, and Google attempts to enforce them as best they can when dealing with millions of videos. They rely on the YouTube user community to assist them in flagging and removing inappropriate content.

By following the search suggestions laid out in this chapter, you won't very likely run into objectionable content. But if you do there is a way to "flag" it to alert YouTube so they can take action to remove it if deemed inappropriate.

Watch this quick video to learn how to flag content that violates YouTube's guidelines and help keep YouTube a safe surfing environment.

VIDEO: *Flagging on YouTube: The Basics*
http://youtu.be/ZA22WSVlCZ4

Searching for Videos

YouTube has changed dramatically since the first edition of this book. As is true with many of the Google tools, signing into YouTube with your free Google account gives you access to the full range of features, including subscribing to your favorite video channels, creating groups of your favorite videos called playlists, and even creating your own YouTube channel. Let's start with finding videos. It's pretty easy to do because YouTube sports the same powerful Google search engine.

Search YouTube by typing keywords and phrases into the search box and click the Search button. You can use the same search operators we've already covered in the earlier chapters of this book.

Once you have conducted an initial search, the Filters button will become available to you. Click the down arrow to reveal more search options. (*Image below*)

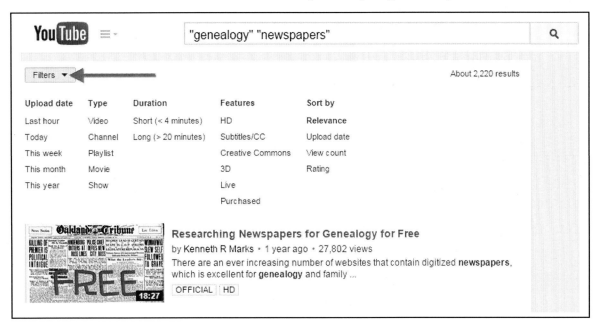

Here you can narrow your search by:
- the date the video was uploaded. (Options include anytime, this month, this week, or today. This can help you locate newly uploaded videos without having to wade through all of them.)
- the type of content you are looking for such as an individual video, a YouTube channel, a playlist, show (YouTube partners with television shows and video producers who deliver content in a series format,) and movies (Full-length movies and trailers.)
- video length (less than 4 minutes, 4-20 minutes, or longer than 20 minutes.)
- special video features such as HD, or closed captioning.

You can also sort your results list by:
- Relevance
- Upload Date
- View Count
- Rating

When you click one of these filters, YouTube will rerun the search and update your results. Your applied filters will appear at the top of the list. (*Image next page*) You can remove a filter by clicking the "x" next to it.

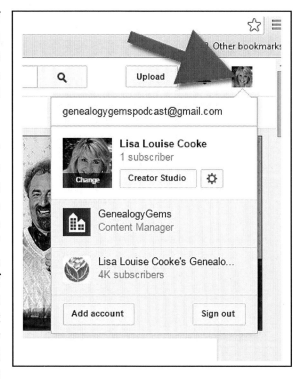

Navigating Your Way through YouTube

With any luck you will soon have a number of videos that are of interest to you, and YouTube offers ways to keep things manageable and interactive. All of these management tools require that you be signed in to your YouTube account.

Once you are signed in you will see your account name in the upper right corner of the screen. Even as I write this I can see changes on the horizon. Currently you can have more than one channel, and YouTube appears to be working on a new "Content Manager" dashboard which looks like it will become the hub of activity for folks who publish lots of videos on YouTube channels. This may remain a separate area for your account profile or it may all merge together. One thing we know for sure about working online is that it will inevitably change. So as we move through this chapter, please beware that while things may have moved by the time you sit down to read this, the overarching concepts stay more constant. In this case, when I say "click your account" in the upper right corner (*image above*), you may find yourself clicking something called Content Manager. The functionality will be in the same sphere (managing your account) but will likely be expanded.

Your videos, playlists and subscriptions can be found by clicking the button with the three lines next to the YouTube logo. This is also known as "settings" or "customization." (*Image right*) Again, buttons like this one are known to move around on websites, but typically you'll find it somewhere along the top of the page.

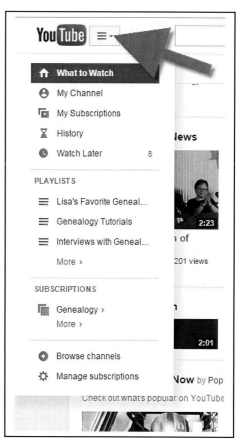

What to Watch (Your Home Page on YouTube)
This first item has a small house icon next to it to signal that you will be taken to your home page on YouTube. The page includes:

- Video recommendations for you based on your previous video viewing.
- A row for each YouTube channel that you currently subscribe to and the most current videos those channels have published.
- Playlists of the most popular videos currently on YouTube in various categories such as music, films, and sports.
- Channels that YouTube recommends for you based on your viewing habits.

Also in this top section under *What to Watch* you will find links to:

- *My Channel* - We will talk more about creating your own YouTube channel later in this chapter.
- *My Subscriptions* - Here you can also view the latest uploads from your favorite channels as well as manage your channel subscriptions.
- *History* – Here you can see what you have been watching and searching for on YouTube. This is handy when you want to find a video you watched a few days ago. Notice that there are buttons at the top of this page that allow you to control when history is on, and clear your viewing history.
- *Watch Later* – This feature is relatively new and one of the best things YouTube has added in a long time. When you come across a video that you are interested in but don't have time at the moment to watch, click the plus sign under the video and click the Watch Later box. (*Image right*) YouTube will add it to your Watch Later list. This has done wonders for helping me stay focused on the research at hand, and I'm guessing you will benefit too!

Playlists

The next section of options is Playlists. A playlist is a collection of videos that share a common tag. If you are brand new to YouTube it will be empty. An easy way to begin is to create a playlist for each category of genealogy-themed videos that we discussed at the beginning of this lesson such as:

- Historical Events / Vintage Footage
- Family History Documentaries
- Genealogy Instructional Videos
- Archives, Libraries, & Repositories
- Genealogy Experts and Vendors Interviews
- Family History Fun

How to Create a Playlist:

1. Click the Settings button. (*Image below*)
2. Click Playlists.
3. Click the + New Playlist button

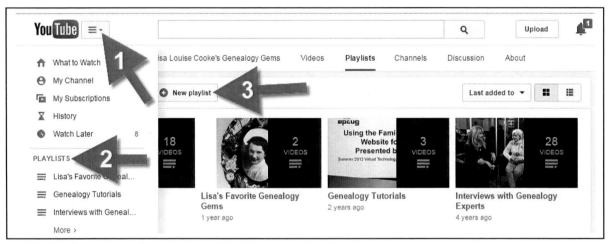

4. In the pop up box type a title for your playlist.
5. From the drop down menu select from Public (viewable by all), Unlisted (viewable only with a direct link), or Private (viewable only by you.)
6. Click the Create button.

> **QUICK TIP:** If you start to collect a number of videos of events and vintage film footage, consider creating a playlist for each of the surnames you are researching and add the videos to the appropriate family playlist. You can always delete playlists, so play with them until you have playlists that support your research in the best and most organized way.

After clicking the Save button you will now be on the page for the newly created playlist within your account. Here you can manage the videos in your playlist and share them with others if you wish. Click the Playlist Settings button for all your options.

There are a couple of different options for adding videos to your playlist.

Option 1: from Playlists in your account:

1. Click the Settings button (upper left corner.)

2. Click the desired playlist from the list of Playlists.
3. Click Add Video button.
4. Locate the desired video by searching for it, copying and pasting the video's URL, or selecting from videos already uploaded to your own channel.

Option 2: from any video on YouTube:
1. Locate an individual video in YouTube.
2. Click the "Add to" (plus sign) underneath the video.
3. Click to select the playlist to which you want it added.

See It for Yourself: Learn more about Playlists
VIDEO: *How to Make a Playlist on YouTube*
http://youtu.be/LPDKqadQEP8

Liked Videos
As you're searching YouTube you will probably come across interesting videos that you like but that don't quite fit into a particular Playlist. Those videos are good candidates to be marked as "Liked" (formerly known as "Favorites").

You'll find the thumbs up "Liked" icon under each video. Click it and the thumb will turn blue. You'll also see a brief blue bar at the top of the video indicating that you just added that video to your Liked playlist. Every YouTube account automatically has a Like Videos playlist. To locate your Liked Videos in your account, click the Settings button and you'll find it under Playlists. (*Image below*)

If you decide that you would like to add the newly liked video to a playlist, just head back to the video's webpage, click the plus sign under the video, and click to select a Playlist.

Video Sharing
Just like uploading your family tree to a genealogy website, sharing your family history videos can be a creative way to connect with other researchers around the world who are researching the same family lines.

Your video must meet the following requirements for uploading to YouTube. Your video must be:

- Less than 15 minutes. (This limit can be increased. Learn more at https://support.google.com/youtube/answer/71673?hl=en or click "Help" at the bottom of any page, and search "video size limit")
- In an acceptable file format (YouTube has added more acceptable formats including .MOV, .MPEG4, .MP4, .AVI, .WMV, .MPEGPS, .FLV, 3GPP, and WebM)

How to Upload a Video to YouTube:

1. Click the Upload button in the upper right corner of any YouTube page.
2. Click the Browse button to browse your computer hard drive for the video file you want to upload (you can upload up to 10 at one time.)
3. Click to select your privacy setting. Choose from public, unlisted, private, or scheduled.
4. Click the Upload Video button to start the uploading process.
5. As the video is uploading, enter information about your video in the fields provided. The more information you provide, the easier it will be for other users to find and watch your video.
6. Click the Save Changes button to save the updates you've made to the video file.

See It for Yourself: Learn more about uploading your own videos
VIDEO: *How to upload a video to YouTube 2014*
http://youtu.be/oZvBuqRxaPs

A Sample Search

Like with all the other searches we've done so far, the place to start is to determine what it is you want to find. Develop a list of keywords, phrases, and data to draw from as you conduct and refine your search.

For this example, I'd like to find some vintage film footage of towns in England where the Cooke ancestors lived. First stop will be the seaside town of Margate, Kent where they owned a hotel in the in late 19th and early 20th centuries.

Here's a list of terms that may come in handy as I attempt to find these types of videos:
- Vintage
- Film
- Footage
- Reel

It's also a good idea to take a quick look at a map and make a list of some of the towns and location names adjoining and associated with Margate:
- Ramsgate

- Thanet
- Cliftonville
- Broadstairs
- Kent

Here's my first search attempt: *Margate film footage*

At first glance the results don't look very promising. But upon closer inspection of the nearly 40 results there are a few possibilities worth looking into:
- Margate in the 1950s & 1960s (a little later than I wanted, but worth noting)
- Memories of Dreamland Margate ("rare footage")
- Ramsgate Life on Film_Part 1

A quick click on *Ramsgate Life* (http://www.youtube.com/watch?v=TnoqGlRIPK8) and within the first few moments of the video it says 1920 – 2009. Soon it launches into quite old footage. A look at the Description box gives more information about what I can expect to see in this video:

> *"I have made an all-new film documenting the events of a fantastic place in Thanet. This extraordinary footage shows events from HMS Thanet's arrival in Ramsgate Harbor in 1919, to visits from Royalty and Ramsgate in War time..."*

This sounds like a good match, and a click of the plus sign beneath the video allows me to add this video to my *Cooke* playlist for later review.

Once you find a video that is of interest to you, capitalize on it! It may lead you to more videos that fit your criteria. You've heard the saying "where there's smoke, there's fire." Well, that is often the case on YouTube.

How to Find Similar Content Based on a Found Video:

1. Related Videos

Check the Related Videos column on the right side of the video page. YouTube automatically groups videos based on their keywords and tags. In this case Parts 2 & 3 of "Ramsgate Life" are listed, as well as a video called "Ramsgate Remembered." The screen shots of the videos allow you to quickly scan them for those vintage black and white images we would be interested in. (*Image right*)

By scrolling through the Related Videos we also come across a video called *British Pathe Archive* that looks like vintage footage. Pathe was a very early film company and would be a good term to add to our keyword search list since there are likely other videos available from the Pathe Archive.

2. Related Users

There's also a good chance that the user who uploaded this video may have uploaded others that we would find interesting. By clicking the linked user's name (*image previous page*), we are taken to their YouTube channel where we can then browse all of their uploaded videos.

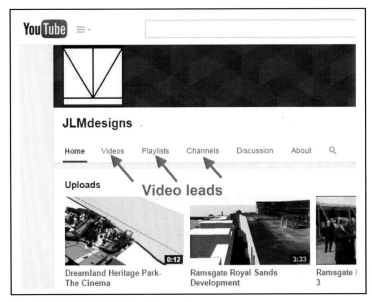

According to the description of the video, this user seems very interested in the Ramsgate area. So once we arrive at their channel, we may also want to view their Videos, Playlists, and Channels lists for possible video leads. (*Image right*)

The bottom line: Everything on YouTube is interconnected. Traditional search is only half the search. The other half is following the links for content that interests you to other related content.

To continue this search for old footage of the Margate area, I might try different combinations of the keywords and locations, incorporating traditional operators as needed to focus in on the videos I want.

Let's try another search on a different subject and find some videos that will help us prepare for a visit to the Allen County Library in Fort Wayne, Indiana.

Initial Search: "Allen County Library"
Results: 96
One of the top results is a video called *Genealogy Center, Allen County Public Library* (http://www.youtube.com/watch?v=tcqDqc0SXgo). By clicking on the user's name we find this video was actually uploaded by the Allen County Library and is one of 120 that they have on their YouTube channel. There is plenty to explore there!

Revised Search: "Allen County Library" "family history"
Results: 58
There are several videos here that look applicable:

Tour of Allen County Public Library: http://youtu.be/zwPx61I4eVg
This Week in America, Curt Witcher Part 2: http://youtu.be/OkBegNVby-4

By clicking on each of these videos and exploring the listed related videos and the user channels we can find our way to more and more relevant videos, many of which we may want to add to our *Archives, Libraries, & Repositories* playlist.

QUICK TIP: Do a search for the words "historic cemetery" and you will find over 2,700 videos! Better yet, type in the name of the cemetery where your ancestors are buried. You might just be surprised at what you find! Then try the same for the churches they attended.

Creating Your Own YouTube Channel

Whether you want to upload single video or become the next viral video superstar, creating your own YouTube channel is fast and easy.

How to Create a YouTube Channel:
1. Sign in to YouTube with your Google account.
2. In the upper right corner, click the blue icon next to the Upload button.
3. Click Creator Studio button.
4. Click Create a Channel.
5. If you are creating your channel for your genealogy society or your business, click "to use a business name" link, and enter your society name, select a category, check terms of service, and click Done. Note: this process will also create a Google+ social network channel, which is beneficial to optimizing your channel's visibility and for search engine optimization (SEO). In other words, it helps your YouTube channel show up higher in search results.
6. When your channel is created you will be returned to the Creator Studio (*image below*), your channel's dashboard where you manage all the elements of your YouTube channel.

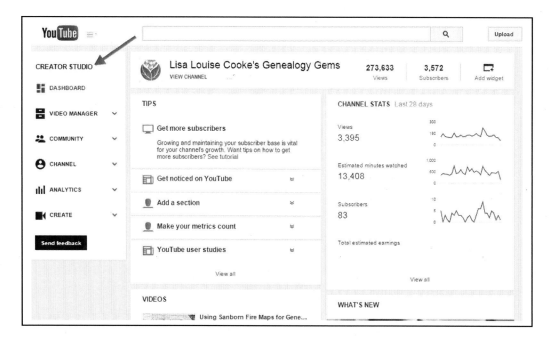

Before you start uploading videos, take a few minutes to customize the settings on your channel under Channel Settings.

How to Customize Your YouTube Settings:

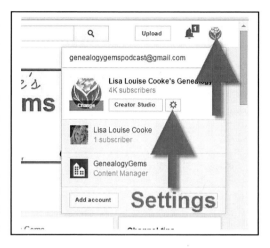

1. In the upper right corner, click the icon again and in the pop up window click the gear icon for Settings. (*Image right*)
2. On this page you can add your organization logo image, your photo, or any other image you want to use to represent your channel. (The recommended image size is 800 x 800 pixels, and no larger than 1 MB.)
3. Copy your unique mobile upload email address that appears on this page and add to your email account / contacts. You can use this to upload videos from your smart phone or tablet.
4. Under Connected Accounts you can connect your channel to your other social media accounts such as Facebook.
5. Under Privacy Settings you can control who sees your videos, playlists, and likes. You can start with 'private' until you're ready to go public.
6. Under Email Settings take time review all the options. I recommend receiving all viewer email until you get a feel for the volume. This is a social network after all.
7. Playback and Connected TVs are for your use as a viewer.
8. Head back to your Creator Studio by clicking your use icon in upper right corner.

Branding Your Channel

If you are creating a channel for your genealogy society, you will want to create a look and feel for your channel that matches your society website, logo and other visual elements. This is called branding, and it helps viewers recognize your channel as an extension of your society. Even if you are creating a channel just for your own personal use, it can still be helpful, and fun, to create a visual look that represents you and your family history on the web.

How to Add Artwork:

1. Go to the Creator Studio and click the View Channel link.
2. Click Add Channel Art button.
3. Upload your artwork (Recommended size 2560 x 1440, 2 MB max.)
4. You'll see how the artwork will look across all computing devices. Make adjustments if needed by clicking the Adjust the Crop button or altering your artwork.
5. When satisfied, click the Select button.
6. If in the future you want to edit your artwork, hover your mouse over the image and click the 'pen' / 'edit' icon.

How to Customize Your Channel Description:

1. Go to the Creator Studio and click the View Channel link.

2. Click About.
3. Click Change Channel Description.
4. Type a keyword rich description in the description box that explains why viewers should invest their time at your channel and what they will get out of it.
5. Enter relevant keywords and phrases that apply to your channel, and that potential viewers will be searching for such as *genealogy*, *family history* and surnames from your family tree.
6. Click the Done button.
7. Add your email address for inquiries by viewers.

How to Add Website Links:
1. Go to the Creator Studio and click the View Channel link.
2. Hover your mouse over the area where you see Google+ and click the Edit (pen icon) in the upper right corner of that section.
3. Your Google+ link will already be listed. Click the Add button.
4. Enter and name each link (i.e. homepage, customer service, Facebook page, etc.)

How to Claim a Custom URL for Your Channel:
Once you get 500 subscribers your channel will qualify for a custom URL address.
1. Go to Settings (click your logo in the upper right corner and click the gear icon.)
2. Under your channel name click the Advanced link.
3. Under Channel Settings click Create Custom URL.
4. In the URL box enter the URL words you want. For example, for my channel I entered the words *Genealogy Gems* and my new customer URL became ***www.youtube.com/GenealogyGems.***
5. YouTube will alert you if another channel has already claimed the name you want.
6. When you're done, click the Create URL Channel button.

Video Success

YouTube has the potential to connect you with other genealogists researching your family tree, and gives you an exciting platform for sharing family history with family and friends. For genealogy societies, it's a wonderful way to provide future members with valuable information. A viewer may just be looking for a few quick answers, but if you show them your expertise, they will return to you when they are ready to join. And if you are interested in starting your own genealogy business, your YouTube channel can be an extremely effective marketing tool. No matter what your goals are, here are keys to YouTube success.

Video Success Requires:
- *Creating great usable content, period!* Build a relationship with your viewers and you will be the one they turn to and buy from.

- *Asking yourself, 'What do my viewers want to know?'* Your job is to create videos that answer those questions.
- *Being authentic.* Your persona is part of your "brand." It will not appeal to everyone and that's OK. You are speaking to a targeted genealogy audience. However, in-person interaction is different than video interaction. You won't have the energy that naturally occurs between two people, so you need to produce and convey that energy all by yourself. It's not false; it's just amped up a bit.
- *Keeping it short.* If possible, keep your videos to a maximum of ten minutes. Three to five minutes is even better.
- *Keeping it simple.* Resist the temptation to do everything in one video. Focus on:
  - → *The Attention Grabbing Opener.* Grab them in the first 10 seconds.
  - → *The Meaty Middle.* Get to the heart of what's really important and provide usable information. If you are using your channel for a business or society, don't be afraid to share your information. Sharing concrete information won't make them go it alone. Rather, it will convince them that they want to be part of your society, or to use your services.
  - → *The Call to Action Closer.* Your viewers aren't mind readers. Tell them what you want them to do! For example, if you would like them to subscribe to your channel so that they will have access to your upcoming videos, ask them to click the Subscribe button on your channel.
- *Investing in lighting.* If you plan on being on camera or doing other live filming, lighting, even minimal inexpensive lighting, can make a big difference in the quality of your videos. To learn more, there is an excellent tutorial video called *Lighting Fundamentals* at the YouTube Creator Academy Channel at http://youtu.be/1Po09zbrfu8.
- *Video editing tools.* You don't have to spend a lot of money to create family history videos. Here are free and fee tools:
  - → Free: Windows Movie Maker at http://windows.microsoft.com/en-us/windows-live/movie-maker.
  - → Free: iMovie at https://www.apple.com/mac/imovie/. (Mac)
  - → Free: Jing at http://www.techsmith.com/jing.html for screen capture. (Mac or PC)
  - → Camtasia (PC) – Download a free trial at http://techsmith.com/camtasia.html. Approximate cost: $299. Screen capture and video production.
  - → Final Cut Pro X (Mac) Download a free trial at http://apple.com/finalcutpro/. Approximate cost: $299.

10 Strategies That Get Views

If you are going to make an effort to share your family history online through video, you certainly will want them to reach your intended audience. Here are some of the things you can do to improve the chances of your videos getting viewed.

1. Link to Your Website in Your Channel and Video Descriptions

If you have a genealogy website, you will definitely want your YouTube channel to lead genealogists to it. You'd be amazed how many folks neglect to put a link to their website in the descriptions of their channel and videos. And don't forget to add it to your channel's "About" section too! (*Image below*)

2. Search Engine Optimization (SEO)

SEO applies to videos as well as websites. Take advantage of the text space in each video description by including relevant keywords and phrases such as "genealogy," "family history," surname, and other words applicable to your family history. (*Image below*) Concentrate your keywords in the beginning of the first paragraph

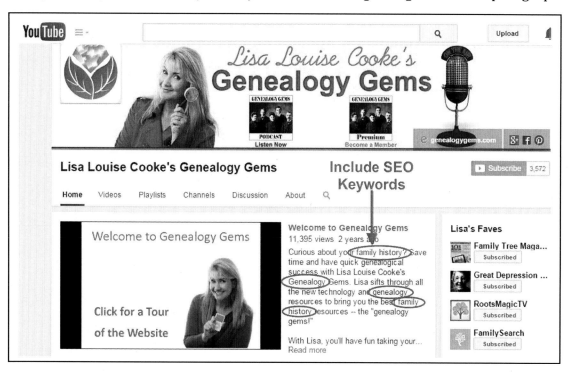

so they will be visible from your channel's homepage. Keywords and phrases should also be included in your video titles. Ask yourself, "what would genealogists interested in my family history or topic be searching for?" Then include those words throughout your channel.

3. Catch and Keep

By default, after your video finishes playing, a variety of thumbnail images of similar topic video will populate the video player. Notice that most of them are not your videos. Once the viewer you worked so hard to attract clicks on one of those thumbnails they will be taken away from your YouTube channel. There is a simple solution to keep viewers on your channel. Once you have finished editing your video, but before you render it (create your final video file) there is one thing left to do. Add 60 seconds to the end of it. Create the final title slide that you want them to be left with, and then drag it over your video editor timeline so that it stays on the screen for at least 60 seconds. Let the sound and or music come to a stop – it gives the impression that the video has ended. But your final slide will still be there giving them the all-important "call to action" (such as "please subscribe to my video channel"), your website URL, and other possible contact information. After a few seconds they will have figured out the next thing they want to do – whether it is to go to your site, click another video from your playlists, etc. Chances are they will move on to the next action of their choice – hopefully the action you suggest in your final slide – and they won't be around long enough to ever see the thumbnails appear on the screen.

4. Select or Create Thumbnail Images for Your Videos
Select your video's thumbnail image, or upload your own. Here's how:
   1. At the top of your channel, click Video Manager.
   2. Click Edit for the video.
   3. Click on the desired thumbnail, or click the Custom Thumbnail button and select an image (up to 2MB) from your computer hard drive.
   4. Click the Save Changes button.
   5. The thumbnail may take several minutes to update on your video page.

5. Ask for What You Want
Ask visitors to click the Subscribe button on your YouTube channel. The Subscribe button is the number one tool for bringing viewers and potential clients back to your channel (and therefore your website) again and again. Once they are subscribed, YouTube will email them a prompt and link each time you upload a new video. And ask them to share your videos via social media.

6. Embed Videos on Your Website
If you have a genealogy blog or website, you can include (also known as embedding) your published videos.

How to Add a Video to a Webpage:
   1. Go to the video page in YouTube.
   2. Click Share. (*Image right*)
   3. Click Embed.
   4. Click on the embed code (HTML code automatically generated by YouTube) to highlight it and press Control + C on your keyboard to copy the code to your computer's clipboard.
   5. Go to your website.
   6. In source code view, paste (Control + V) the code.
   7. When you publish your webpage, the video will appear.
   8. If you have several videos consider creating a Video page on your website. See an example at www.genealogygems.com and click "Genealogy Gems Channel" tab under Video in the menu.

7. Share Links to Your Videos on Message Boards as Part of Your Answer

Rather than posting answers that are blatant commercials for your business or society, post knowledgeable answers that include a link to one of your videos. Once at your YouTube channel they will be prompted to Subscribe, visit your website, join, and hopefully, get involved.

How to Share a Video Link:

1. Go to your video's page on YouTube.
2. Click Share under the video. (*Image below*) A share options box will appear.
3. Click the video's URL to highlight it, and press Control + C on your keyboard to copy it to your computer's clipboard.
4. Press Control + V to paste the URL to share it.

8. Send Video Links with Press Releases

Producing regular valuable content is an ongoing chore for genealogy societies. Make it easy for others to talk about your society by not only sending relevant, well written press releases when you do something noteworthy, but by also including a link and the embed code to a great video.

9. Re-purpose Your Content

For really awesome SEO traction consider transcribing your video and using it to fill your video's description text box. The text will be searchable by Google making it easier for your video to be found, and will add value for your visitors.

10. **My final killer strategy (and for some serious fun!):**
    Don't Underestimate the Power of Cats in Your Videos!
    Video: *Iggy Investigates an iPad* at http://youtu.be/Q9NP-AeKX40
    Video: *Catvertising* at https://www.youtube.com/watch?v=IkOQw96cfyE

More Keys to Success

- **Make use of your free account.**
  Create playlists to organize your videos and research. Mark the videos you like, particularly if they are about a town, cemetery, family, or other research topic that you are interested in. Remember: when other users follow links that interest them they may very well end up on your playlist or channel. When they find videos you've liked they will know you are interested in that family or topic as well, and they may leave a comment that could lead to a research connection.

- **Keep an open mind.**
  The number of genealogical topics that might appear in a YouTube video is only limited by your imagination.

- **Set up Google Alerts for videos.**
  Flip back to Chapter 7 and follow the instructions to set up an alert, but this time select Video from the Sources list. Google will do the searching and alert you by email when a new video meeting your criteria has been uploaded.

CHAPTER 15
Google Earth: An Overview

URL: http://earth.google.com

Google describes the Google Earth tool this way: "Google Earth lets you fly anywhere on Earth to view satellite imagery, maps, terrain, 3D buildings, from galaxies in outer space to the canyons of the ocean. You can explore rich geographical content, save your toured places, and share with others."

From a genealogist's perspective, however, Google Earth offers so much more than virtually flying to locations around the world. It has the power to document your ancestors' lives in a multi-media fashion. And it lends itself very well to collaboration with other researchers and sharing your family history with your loved ones. In this chapter we will explore Google Earth as a 360-degree, 3-dimensional way to view your ancestor's world.

Google Earth is different from the other Google tools because it is software that you install on your computer. However, like all Google tools, the standard version of Google Earth is absolutely free (and that's very uncommon for high powered geographic software.)

You will notice when you go to the download page that they also offer Google Earth Pro. This is the advanced version geared for businesses and currently runs $400. For genealogy however, you will have everything you need in the free version.

How to Download and Install Google Earth:
1. Go to http://earth.google.com.
2. Click the blue Download Google Earth button.

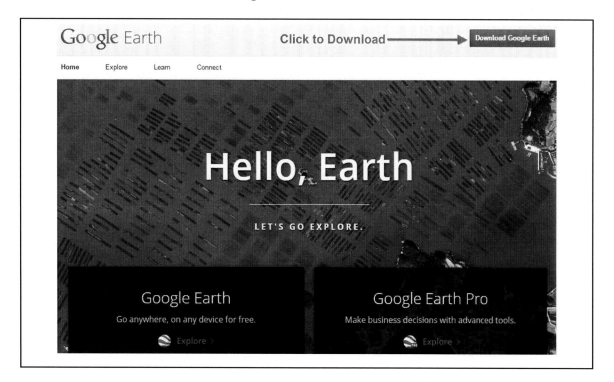

From the Install Google Earth with Google Updater page:

3. Unclick the Include Google Chrome box if you don't wish to install the Google Chrome browser.
4. Read the Terms and Conditions.
5. If you agree to them, click the Agree and Download button.
6. Follow the installation guide.
7. When complete click the Run Google Earth button.
8. The installer will automatically instal a Google Earth icon (*Image right*) on your desktop. Click it to launch the program in the future.

Each time you open Google Earth the Tip box will appear and provide tips for using the program. These can help you get up to speed quickly. If you want to scroll through a number of tips just click the Prev Tip and Next Tip buttons in the bottom left corner. If you don't wish to have the Tip box appear at the start, uncheck the *Show tips at startup* box. (*Image below*)

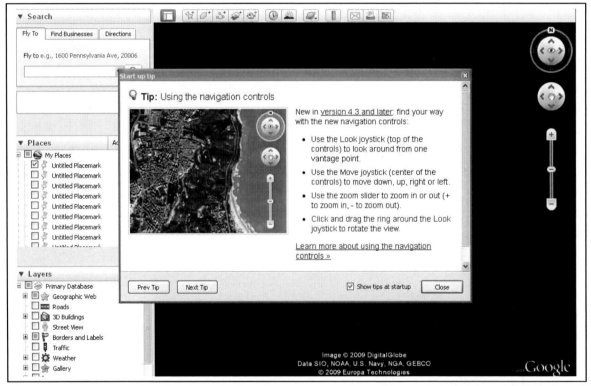

Before you get started using Google Earth, return to your internet browser, which should be opened to Google Earth's *Thank You* page. This page appears after software installation. There are often some good resources here to take note of:

- A tour of 3D buildings in the Google Earth Gallery
- The Google Earth Sightseer Newsletter
- Earth Plug-in for your internet browser

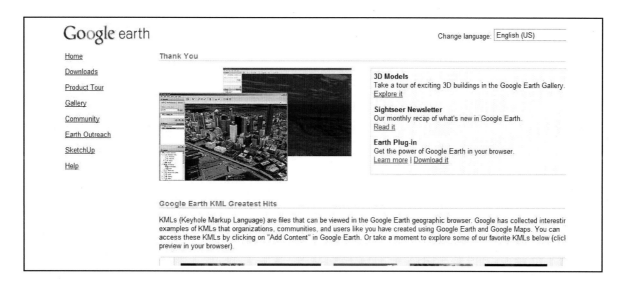

And finally if you cross down to the bottom of the Thank You page you'll find links to some recommended Google Earth blogs with additional tips and ideas.

The Software

Google Earth requires an internet connection to operate. The faster the connection, the better the results you will experience. If Google Earth appears to stop working, look in the bottom right corner and see if a small blue circle is spinning. This means that Google Earth is busy processing your last request, and attempting to display it on the screen. Many of the tasks that Google Earth performs are actually quite complicated and data "heavy." Many times, simply waiting a few moments is all it takes for it to resume running.

Navigation

Across the top of the main screen called the "3D Viewer" is a toolbar. (*Image below*) Hover your mouse over a toolbar button and you will see the label telling you the button's function. They are:

- Hide Side Panels
- Add Placemark
- Add Polygon
- Add Path
- Add Image Overlay
- Record A Tour
- Show Historical Imagery

- Show sunlight across landscape
- Switch between Earth, Sky and Planets
- Show Ruler
- Email
- Print
- View in Google Maps

There is a new button on the toolbar since the last edition of this book. You will find the "Save Image" button between Print and View in Google Maps. (*Image right*) This fulfills a request that I hear from my students on a regular basis. You can now instantly create a JPEG image of whatever appears on your screen while using Google Earth and save it to your computer. This new feature will make including your customized maps in your family history easier than ever.

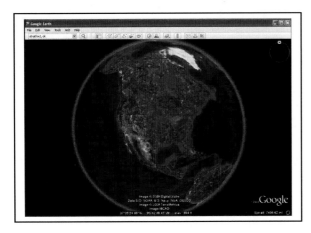

While working in Google Earth you will probably want to keep these panels visible. However, they can be closed to create a larger viewing area (*Image left*) by clicking the Hide Side Panels button on the far left end of the toolbar.

In the upper right corner of the 3D Viewer you will find the Navigation Controls. (*Image below, right*) These let you zoom in and out, and move around.

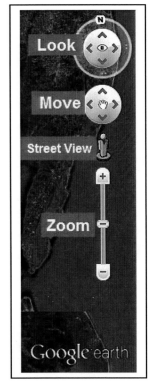

Google Earth does not require north be at the top. Click and drag the ring around the top button to rotate the view. The "N" ring around the top Navigation button controls direction. Whenever you want to return north to the top of the viewer simply click the "N" button to reset the view.

The center of the top button looks like an eye, and is referred to as the Look joystick. Use it to look around from a single vantage point, just like if you were turning your head. After clicking an arrow on the Look joystick, move the mouse around on the joystick to change the direction of motion.

The middle button is the Move joystick, which allows you to move your position on the Earth from one place to another. Click an arrow on Move to look in that direction and then move the mouse around on the joystick to change the direction of motion.

Beneath the Move joystick is Street View. Click on the yellow icon and drag it over the map. Blue lines will appear to indicate which streets have Street View available. (Note: If you don't see the Street View icon you are not zoomed in close enough.) Drop the icon directly on to the blue line where you want to see Street View. If you don't drop it on a blue line, you will only achieve "Ground-Level View" which typically features a blurry ground and a night sky. Click "Exit Ground-level view" to return to satellite view and start again.

When you do achieve Street View, you can navigate by:
- using the arrow keys on your keyboard.
- by clicking on the viewer further down the street.
- clicking and dragging the displayed image.

We will be discussing Street View in more depth as we move through the upcoming chapters on Google Earth.

On the bottom of the Navigation Controls you will find the zoom slider. This allows you to zoom in and out by moving the slider handle or by clicking the plus and minus signs. As you move closer to the ground, Google Earth tilts to change your viewing angle to be parallel to the Earth's surface.

You can also navigate quickly and easily by using:

The Arrow Keys on your keyboard.
- Page Up and Page Down keys will drive you faster.
- Holding the ALT key down along with the Arrow Keys will move you more slowly.
- Holding the Control key (or Command key in Mac) down along with the Up or Down arrows will tilt your view.

Your mouse:
- Use the scroll wheel on your mouse (if it has one) to "drive" forward and backward.
- Click and drag the screen to move around and change directions.
- Double-click on any location in front of you to fly directly there. Two clicks zooms in, and two right-clicks zooms out. To stop the zoom, just click once on the viewer.

Learn more about navigating in Google Earth
VIDEO: *Navigating in Google Earth*
http://www.youtube.com/watch?v=rd2uXE1fTI0

Panels
Along the left side of your screen (*image right*) you'll find three panels: Search, Places, and Layers.

Search Panel
To find a geographic location, just type the name, address, or latitude and longitude in the Fly To search box, and click the Search button. (*Image right*) For example, you could enter the name of a town or state, a zip code, or any other location-based search query as in the example in the image below. If Google Earth finds multiple possible matches it will list them in the box below so that you can select the one you want.

You will notice that the results look much more like Google search results than they used to. That's a welcome improvement since I wrote the first edition of this book. The places you search will remain listed in the box, available to be returned to with a click. To clear the searches from the box, click the X in the bottom right corner of the Search panel box. (*Image right*)

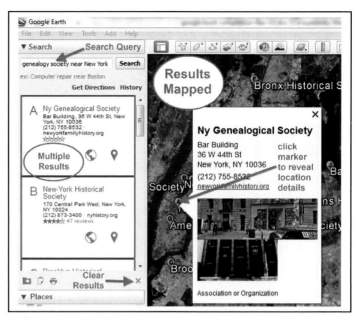

Click the hyperlinked title to zoom in to the location. If the location has an accompanying website, there is no need to open a separate web browser in order to view it. Simply click the globe in the result listing in the Search panel to open the website in Google Earth. (*Image below*)

Also in the Search panel you can get directions from one location to another.

How to Get Directions:
1. Click *Get Directions.*
2. Enter your *From* location.
3. Enter a *To* location.
4. Click the Get Directions button. (*Image left*)
5. Google Earth will instantly map out the journey turn by turn and plot it on the map. (*Image next page*)

Places Panel

Think of the Places panel as a window to your computer's hard drive. This is where you locate, save, organize, and revisit your placemarks and files. These files are stored deep on your hard drive, and displayed in the Places panel, making them convenient to work with. Your Places panel files can't be seen by anyone else unless you decide to share a file online.

Customized elements that you add to the map (such as placemarks and overlays that we will discuss in upcoming sections of this book) are saved to the Places panel as .KML files. When exported, they are saved as .KMZ which is a zipped file containing one or more elements. KML stands for Keyhole Markup Language, and according to Wikipedia it is defined as "an XML notation for expressing geographic annotation and visualization within Internet-based, two-dimensional maps and three-dimensional Earth browsers." In layman's terms, it is the file type that all Google Earth maps are saved as. Just as a photograph file is a .JPEG, a Google Earth file is a .KML. This file name makes sense when you look into the history of Google Earth, which was originally named "Keyhole Earth Viewer."

If you download a KMZ file from the internet, or receive a file from someone else (for instance, by email) it will open automatically in Google Earth when clicked. The file will appear in the Temporary folder at the bottom of your Places panel. If you wish to save the file to Google Earth, simply drop and drag onto "My Places" at the top of the panel. You can also create a folder in the Places panel and drag and drop it into the folder.

How to Create a Folder in the Places Panel:
1. Right-click My Places. (*Image next page*)
2. Click Add.
3. Click Folder.

4. In the pop up dialog box type a title for your folder.
5. Type in a description if desired.
6. Click OK.
7. The new folder will appear at the bottom of the My Places list.
8. Drag and drop the folder to desired order of files and folders.

If you elect not to save it to a permanent location in My Places, it will be deleted when you close Google Earth. We will discuss file management in more depth later.

There used to be an Add Content button in the Places panel. This has now been moved to the Layers panel, and is called Google Gallery. The Layers panel is a much more logical place for it since it links to online content and not content specific to your computer. Clicking the button takes you to the Google Maps Gallery website containing community-created Google Earth files that you can view using Google Earth or Google Maps. We'll talk more about it in the next section.

Layers Panel

In this book we are going to focus on the Google Earth features that support executing and reporting our genealogy research. While not all the data in the Layers panel will be useful to genealogy, Layers are a key feature of Google Earth and deserve a quick review.

Think of the Layers panel as your window to content on the internet. Layers provide a collection of points of geographic interest that can be displayed in the 3D viewer. You'll find the Layers panel on the bottom left side of your screen. Layers content is created by Google or its content partners and is hosted online, which is one of the reasons why Google Earth requires an internet connection.

To display all points of interest (POIs) within a layer, click the box next to the Layer title.

POIs within the layer can be selected and unselected the same way. To open a Layer category click the plus sign next to the label to open the layer folder, and the minus sign to close the layer folder. (*Image right*)

You will likely want to experiment at some point with all of the available layers, but for now here are some genealogically helpful ones to give particular notice.

Borders and Labels

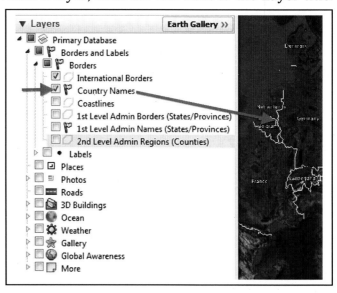

Gallery > Rumsey Historical Maps
- About the Maps
- Map Finder (allows you to lay an available map over a geographic area to see it as it once was)

Gallery > Webcams
- Webcams.travel (allows you to view live shots where available)

More > Place Categories
- Libraries
- Places of Worship (within this category you will find Cemeteries)
- Museums
- Schools

US Boundaries
- City Boundaries
- Postal Code Boundaries

(Note: Many of these POIs could be of interest if you are planning a visit)

> **QUICK TIP:** Each Layer has different requirements on how close you must be zoomed in on a geographic area to be able to view the POIs. For instance, if you're trying to view buildings you will have to be zoomed in close enough for buildings to be seen. If you're having difficulty viewing layers and POIs, zoom in and out until you find what you're looking for.

As I mentioned in the Places panel section, the Google Gallery is a website where customized maps can be uploaded by Google Earth users. An easy way to get started is to explore their historical maps. (*Image below*)

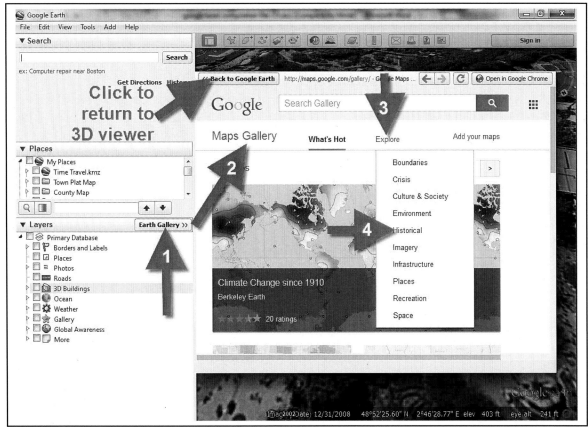

www.GenealogyGems.com

How to Download Maps from the Gallery to Google Earth:
1. In the Layers panel click the Earth Gallery button.
2. The Maps Gallery will open in the 3D viewer.
3. Click Explore in the menu.
4. Click Historical in the drop down menu.
5. Click to select the desired map.
6. Click View in Google Earth.
7. The map will appear in the 3D viewer.
8. You will see the overlay at the bottom of the list in the Layers panel.

The Power of Street View

Google Earth's Street View takes your experience from the high level satellite view to an up close and personal street level view. Street View does more than just allow you to "walk" down streets at street level on the map, it also provides a way to explore world landmarks and natural wonders up close, and step inside locations such as museums, arenas, restaurants and small businesses with 360-degree images.

Launched in May of 2007 by Google, Street View first featured a few major cities in the U.S. Today nearly every street in America is represented in Street View, and it is quickly spreading around the world.

Just how does Google do it? They have developed a fleet of specially adapted cars with nine directional cameras attached to the tops at a height of about 8 feet. These cars drive up and down each street snapping photographs from all directions every few seconds. When faced with narrow streets such as in Rome in Italy, Google Trikes (tricycles) were similarly equipped to make the journey. They've even employed snowmobiles where necessary in cold climate areas!

Street View has undergone a major transformation since the first edition of this book was published. Gone are the individual camera icons. Today, you can simply drag and drop the Street View icon onto the map, and move seamlessly from image to image.

When it comes to genealogy, a real life application is the best way to convey the power of the street view feature in Google Earth. Here's an example of how I used street view to find my Great Grandparents home and store 100 years later and identify a vintage photograph at the same time.

I have had this photo (*image right*) of my great grandfather holding my grandfather in late 1906 in San Francisco for over thirty years, but have never been sure where it was taken. I turned to the 1910 census because it is the closest U.S. Population Schedule available to the year 1906. I extracted the address that the census taker wrote in the left hand margin: *288 Connecticut St.*

The first step in Google earth was to go to the Search panel and Fly to the address. It's important to zoom in close enough to see the street and be able to distinguish building outlines.

As you zoom closer, the Street View "man" icon will appears in the upper right corner of the 3D Viewer above the zoom tool. The Street View icon debuted with Google Earth Version 6.0. (Prior to that Street View was activated in the Layers panel.) Click on the icon and drag and drop it on map. As you drag it over the map, blue lines will appear in locations across the map where Street View is available. Drop the icon directly on to the blue line in the desired location *(Image right: Drag and drop the Street View icon onto the blue lines to access Street View.)*

Visualize yourself standing on the location. By clicking and grabbing the image you can spin around in a complete circle and see everything from that position just as if you were standing there yourself! Notice that Google Earth displays the address where you are "standing." At the bottom of the screen you'll see which direction you are looking (North, South, East, or West.) Grab the image and turn the view to look straight down the road and the name of the street appears in the center of the road. This is very helpful because it is easy to get a bit disoriented. Look for these cues from Google Earth to keep track of where you are.

I zoomed in on the address and used the navigation tools to try to get the same perspective as my original photo. That way I could compare the two side by side to see if it was a match.

To view the street from another position, just double click on that spot on the screen and you will be "transported" there visually with a full 360-degree view. The address of the viewing location will always appear in the upper right corner of the viewer. (*Image right*)

There are other ways to navigate in addition to grabbing and dragging the image. Use the right and left arrows on your keyboard to turn right and left. Use the Up arrow to zoom in and the Down arrow to zoom out. You can exit Street View anytime by clicking the Exit Street View button in the very top right corner of the screen.

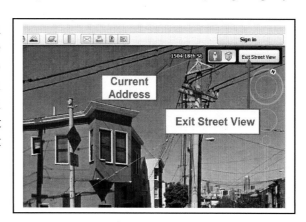

Finding the Location

While the address appears in the upper right corner of the screen as you move through Street View, it does not necessarily reflect the exact address of the location you are viewing. For instance, I can be viewing the building at 288 Connecticut Street, but Street View will be displaying the address across the street or right next store. Therefore, it can be challenging to identify where the exact address location is in the 360-degree Street View. You may need to jump back and forth between Street View and the regular map view to compare landmarks. Locate the address on the regular map. Is there an empty lot next door? A large tree in front? Use the ring around the top "North" navigation button to tilt your view for more comparison. Also keep an eye out for street numbers on curbs and front porches.

Since my case was in San Francisco, I had the added advantage of the hills to help me determine where to look first. You'll notice in my original photo that the road slopes downward in to the distance. This geographic feature helped eliminate two of the four streets I could see from Street View since they both sloped uphill. Of the two remaining streets one sloped far more than the street in the photo, so I decided to examine the other street first.

Using the photo as my guide I looked down the left side of the street, keeping an eye out for any distinguishing building elements. It didn't take long to notice a tall building with a similar roof overhang to the one in the photo. Soon I was able to match up several points on each of the images. (*Image below*)

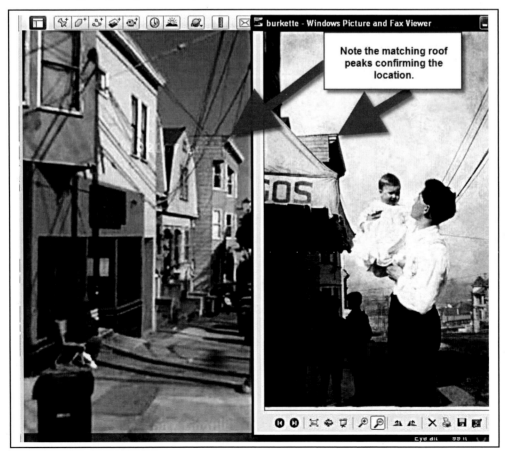

My great grandparents moved several times in the first decade of the 20th century. Google Earth provided the quickest way for visiting the various locations, comparing images, and determining the exact location. Photographs can become a little less mysterious with Google Earth.

See it for Yourself!
Watch my free full length video class **Google Earth for Genealogy**
VIDEO LINK: http://lisalouisecooke.com/free-google-earth-for-genealogy-video-class-by-lisa-louise-cooke/

Ground-Level View and 3D Data

After you activate Street View by clicking, dragging, and dropping the Street View icon onto the map, a mini toolbar will appear in the upper right corner of the 3D Viewer. You can toggle between the Street View icon and the new building icon which represents Ground-Level View. You can also go back to the regular map by clicking the Exit Street View button. (*Image right*)

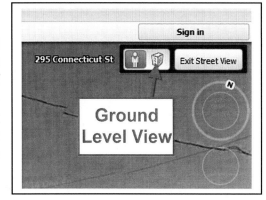

Ground-Level View provides a cool way to see all the 3D data available in Google Earth. The data is provided by Google and the large number of individuals around the world using Google Sketch-Up to create 3D models for Google Earth. To get the most out of Ground-Level View, click the box next to 3D Buildings in the Layers panel to activate them.

In addition to large cities like San Francisco that feature large numbers of 3D buildings in Google Earth, Walt Disney World in Orlando, Florida is a great place to try out the features of Ground-Level View. Type "Epcot Center" in the Fly To box and press enter. Once you have arrived, drag and drop the Street View icon onto the spot on the screen where you want to begin using Street View and Ground-Level View.

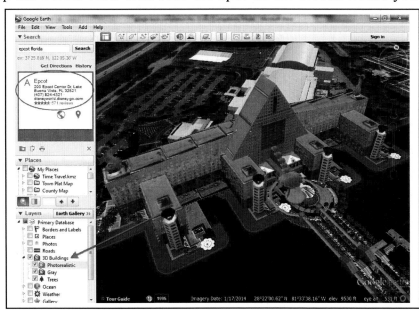

The first thing you will notice is that the buildings and many of the trees are now 3D, but that's just the beginning. Epcot is also unique in that you can actually go inside some buildings (though the contents are incomplete) and by clicking on each feature (rides, hotels, etc.) you will usually get a pop-up window providing you with more information, and even videos!

The Future is Here

In the first edition of this book, I predicted that we would see Ground-Level View expand across the globe. Sure enough, cities, communities and even historic locations are now creating media rich content using Google Earth. (*Image below: Inside Gettysburg National Military Park.*)

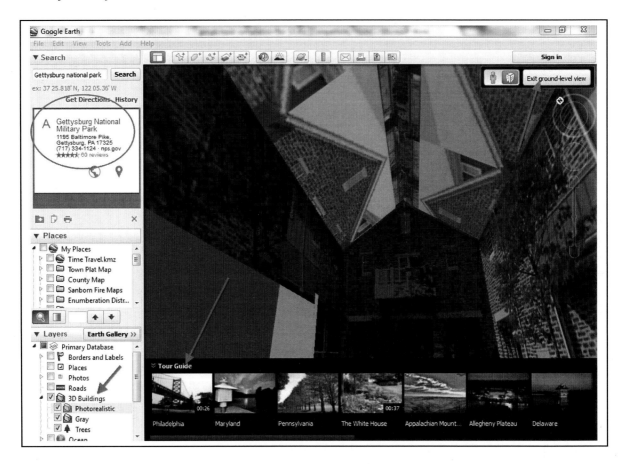

Notice the new "Tour Guide" tab appears at the bottom of the screen. Click it and the photographic Tour Guide bar will appear. If you don't see it, in the menu at the top of your screen go to View and click Tour Guide. As you close in on locations of interest, the Tour Guide will appear, offering you thumbnail images of points of interest. Click one, and you'll be automatically taken on a tour of that site, including a brief description and historical facts. After the tour finishes, click the "x" in the upper corner of the tour player to close it. To disable the tour guide, go back up to the View menu and uncheck Tour Guide.

See it for Yourself
VIDEO: *Learn Google Earth: Tour Guide*
http://youtu.be/CkkqKcN0s30

I have no doubt there is much more in store in the future in Google Earth!

CHAPTER 16
Google Earth: Ancestral Homes & Locations

Geography and genealogy go hand in hand. It's impossible to locate records or accurately follow family lines without understanding boundaries, jurisdictions, land formations, and distances. Decisions that directly affected your family for generations consistently revolve around geography such as:

- Where official records are created
- The path chosen for migration
- Locations selected for settlement
- Division of farms and property in probate

Because land itself doesn't move, it's one of the few elements of our ancestors' lives that we can always count on. Consider an old photograph. Buildings may have changed but the surrounding landmarks such as hills, valleys and rock formations still stand today, and can aid in identification.

(Image above: Charles Burkett gets his photograph taken high atop a pony on the streets of San Francisco, circa 1907)

Placemark Basics

When you are working with the census you can often extract the address of the home where your ancestor lived. Google Earth offers you a powerful way to get an up close and personal view of that location. Here's an example:

According to the 1910 U.S. Federal Population Census, my great grandparents lived at 288 Connecticut St., San Francisco, CA. (*Image right*)

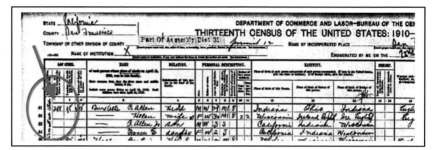

When we type in the complete address in the Fly To box in the Search panel and click the search button, Google Earth will fly to that exact location on the map. Using the navigation controls we can zoom in even closer.

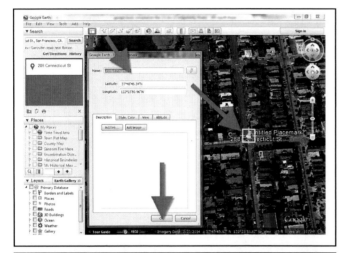

By clicking the Add Placemark button (*image left*) in the toolbar we can mark the exact location on the map. A dialog box appears where we can enter a title for the placemark and a complete description. Clicking the OK button closes the dialog box and saves the placemark.

Each time we click on the pin (*image bottom left*) all of that data will appear in a description balloon.

The saved pushpin file can be found in the Places panel.

We will cover this more in depth with step-by-step instructions throughout these Google Earth chapters.

The home of my Great Grandparents

288 Connecticut St., San Francisco, CA
Directions: To here - From here

The home of my Great Grand

Francisco, CA 94107

Finding Ancestral Homes and Locations

For most researchers it just isn't financially feasible to personally travel to all of the locations where your ancestors lived. The good news is that Google Earth can provide you with a "virtual reality" type

experience that is as close to being there as your computer can take you.

Plot an Ancestor's Home

Let's start with a location that you very likely are familiar with – the house where one of your grandparents lived. If by chance you don't have that address, conduct this exercise for one of your childhood homes.

How to Add a Placemark:
1. In the Search panel type the address in the Fly To box and click the Search button.
2. The globe in the 3D viewer will start to turn and very quickly will zoom in to that location.
3. Click the Placemark button in the toolbar at the top of the 3D viewer to mark the location.

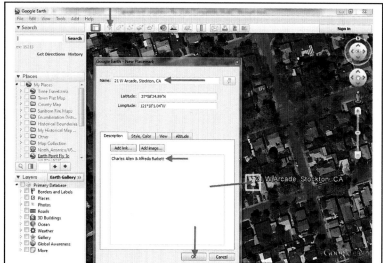

4. When the New Placemark box opens, label the placemark with the exact street address, and in the description type your grandparents' names. (*Image right*)
5. Click OK.

You have now located your first ancestral home on Google Earth. But this is only the beginning...

Getting a Closer Look: Street View

While it is certainly interesting to locate an ancestor's home on the globe, it's difficult to see much detail from high above with Google Earth's satellite view. To get an up close look at a location we will need to employ Google Earth's Street View function.

Start at the ancestor's home you identified in the previous exercise.
1. Click on the Street View icon in the upper right corner of the 3D viewer, and drag him over the map until the blue Street View lines appear.
2. Drop the icon directly on the blue line in the location where you want to begin viewing.
3. Use the arrow keys on your keyboard, or the navigation tools in the upper right corner, to move around within Street View.

It can be a little confusing getting your directional bearings once you are in Street View. Look for the street address in the upper right corner of the 3D viewer (*image next page*), and house numbers on the house as well as the curb. (*Image right*)

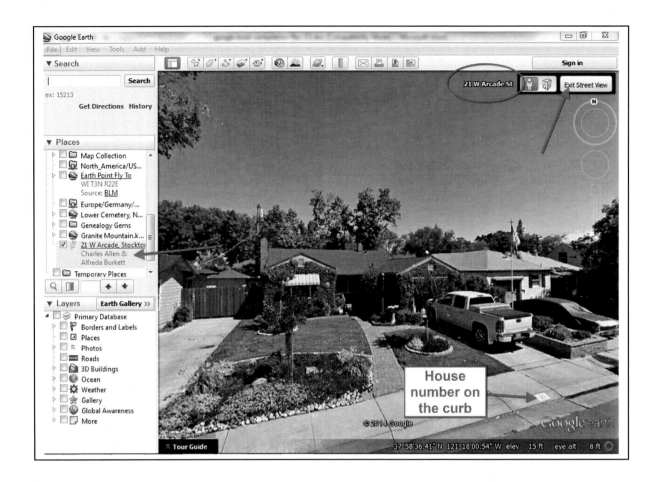

QUICK TIP: In the U.S., even-numbered addresses will typically be on one side, and odd-numbered addresses on the opposite side of the street. If the house you are looking for doesn't have a street number on the house or curb, look to the houses on either side to deduce the correct home.

Exploring Additional Locations

Now that we've located an ancestor's home and explored it up close with Street View, it's time to start pondering other types of family history locations that might be worthy of a virtual visit. Here are some initial ideas for ancestral locations to explore:

- Homes
- Villages
- Farms
- Homesteads
- Businesses
- Photograph Locations
- Places of Worship

...and the list goes on.

You probably have a lot more of these locations at your fingertips than you realize!

Places to look:
- Your genealogy database. Chances are over time you have entered addresses based on the records you've located.
- Original Records.
- Old Address Books.
- Old letters.

Practice Makes Perfect

Select one grandparent and spend some time plotting out locations that were pertinent throughout his or her life. Mark each location with a placemark. (*Image right*)

In the next chapter we will put a plan in place for saving, organizing and sharing those locations, as well as the other places we find. It will be the foundation for your Google Earth treasury of family history geography.

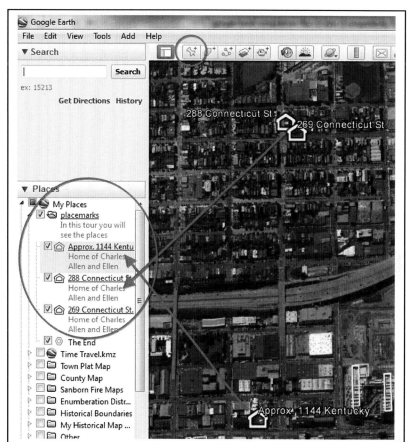

Stay Alert with Follow Your World

http://www.followyourworld.appspot.com

As you work with Google Earth you will notice that some areas still don't have Street View and many areas have fairly outdated satellite view, or no historical aerial view at all. There's always hope that new imagery will come to the areas of the world where you research your family history because Google publishes updates approximately every 30 days.

Wouldn't it be nice if there was a Google Alert for Google Earth so that you would receive a notification if imagery was updated to your ancestor's neck of the woods? Well, there is! It's called Follow Your World.

When you get to the Follow Your World website, click the big blue button on the homepage to log in to your free Google account. On the next page you will see the Google Earth map. Scroll down below the map and follow the instructions on the next page.

How to "Follow" a Google Earth Location:

1. Type in the location you want to follow in the Step 1 field. This can be a specific address, latitude or longitude, or city, state, etc.
2. Click the Search Location button. (*Image below*)

3. Once the location pops up, click on the map and drag the location to center under the cross hairs in the center of the screen. This will mark the exact point for which you want to receive imagery update notifications. (*Image below*)

4. Click the Select Point button to generate the correct latitude and longitude for that exact location.
5. Name the image so that you'll remember why you were interested in the location (i.e. name of town and surname.)
6. Your email notifications will be sent to the email address tied to your Google account.
7. Click the Submit button.

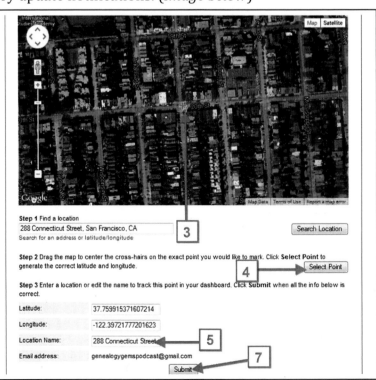

www.GenealogyGems.com

You'll be taken to a thank you page. There you can click the Dashboard link to go to your Follow Your World dashboard. There you can manage your alerts, much like Google Alerts. You can Unsubscribe at any time, as well as delete an alert. If you need to revise a location, simply delete it and create a new Point by clicking the Add New Point button. You can return to your dashboard any time you are signed into your Google account by going to http://www.followyourworld.appspot.com/dashboard.

Now when Google adds new imagery or imagery updates in an area you have pinpointed, you will be among the first to know! (*Image below*)

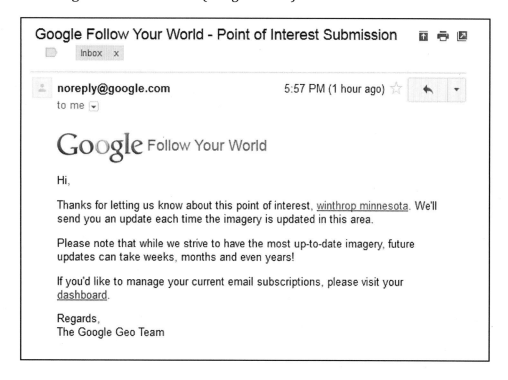

CHAPTER 17
Google Earth: Saving, Organizing, & Sharing

Now that you've explored some ancestral locations in Google Earth, it's a good time to stop and think about organization. As you progress through these chapters you will soon begin to collect locations and information that you will want to keep and easily retrieve. Laying a solid organizational foundation for your work in Google Earth now will pay big dividends down the road.

Placemarks: Creating, Naming, and Organizing

You may have noticed in the previous chapter that each time you added a placemark (the pushpin icon in the toolbar) to the globe it was added to the My Places folder in the Places panel. Look for the yellow pushpin icons in the Places panel. You will notice that if you labeled the placemark when the New Placemark dialog box popped up, the name you entered appears as the name of the pushpin. If you skipped that step, the pushpin will simply be named Untitled Placemark.

How to Create and Name a Placemark:

1. Fly to the location of your choice on the map.
2. Click the Add Placemark button on the 3D Viewer toolbar.
3. Type in a name.
4. Click OK.
5. If you wish to rename the placemark, locate it in the Places panel and right click it.
6. Select Rename.
7. Type in the name.
8. Press the Enter key on your keyboard.

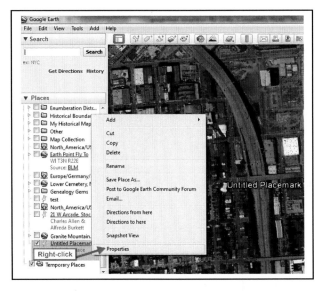

Now you have the flexibility to rename your Placemarks as needed to keep them descriptive and organized. I recommend keeping them brief. Otherwise the text can clutter your view of the map. If you need to say more, type it into the Description section of the placemark. To do so, follow the same procedure above, except when you get to step 7, select Properties (*Image above*) and the Edit Placemark dialog box will appear.

Folders

It doesn't take long after adding a few placemarks to Google Earth to determine that some additional organization will be needed. There is a simple way to avoid piling up all your locations under My Places. Creating folders will help you store and organize your placemarks. Folder management is very much like the folder management you do on your computer's hard drive, except you can do it within Google Earth.

See It For Yourself!
Video: *Organize Your Hard Drive Video*
At the Family Tree Magazine You Tube Channel
Learn the basic concepts of organizing digital family history files on your computer hard drive.

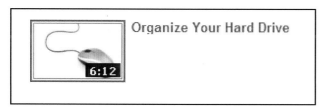

Watch the video at:
http://youtu.be/oWFDITBusPM

In the case of filing your files in Google Earth, I prefer creating surname file folders. Start with the surnames you search the most. Add folders as needed. There is no limit to how many you can have!

How to Create Surname Folders:
1. Click on My Places in the Places panel to highlight it.
2. Right Click to reveal menu options.
3. Select Add > New Folder.
4. The New Folder box will pop up.
5. Name the folder. (i.e. *Smith*, etc. Focus on the surnames you intend to work on first.)
   a. In the Description area type in information that will assist you in understanding the family line this folder refers to. For example, *"The Smith family of Ohio with origins in England. Year of immigration: 1860. Earliest head of household: John T. Smith, person #461 in database."*

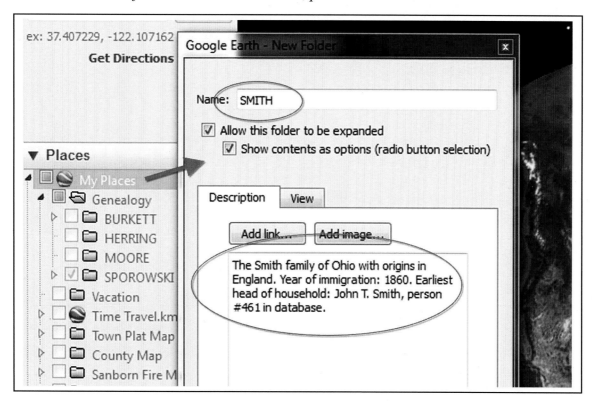

www.GenealogyGems.com

6. Click two check boxes allowing greater visibility in the Places panel:
    a. Allow this folder to be expanded.
    b. Show contents as options.
        (These can always be removed at a later time.)
7. Click OK.

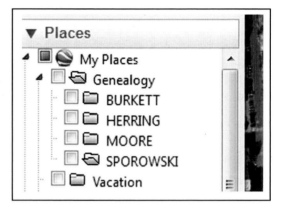

QUICK TIP: If you anticipate using Google Earth for other activities in addition to genealogy, create a Genealogy folder first, and then follow the previous steps to create folders within the Genealogy folder. (*Image right*)

You now have your first surname folder in your Places panel. Go ahead and take a few moments to create a few more just to get comfortable with the process of making folders.

How to Create a Placemark in a Folder:
When you identify a location that you want to mark and save in a particular folder:
1. Click once on the folder in the Places panel to select it. By selecting the folder first, the new placemark will be saved to that folder.
2. Click the Placemark icon in the toolbar.
3. Enter data.
4. Click OK.

How to Move Placemarks Between Folders:
If by chance you end up with a placemark in the wrong folder it can easily be moved:
1. Click to select the placemark in the Places panel.
2. Drag it to the appropriate folder.
3. Drop it into the folder.
Similarly, folders can also be dragged and dropped into other folders.

How to Delete Files or Folders:
Files and folders within the Places panel can be as easily deleted as they are created. To delete a file or an entire folder:
1. Right click on the file or folder to be deleted.
2. Select Delete from the menu.
3. Click OK in the pop up box.

A Final Word
The good news is that manipulating placemarks and folders is easy. That means you're never stuck with a system that is not working for you. Experiment!

Saving Images

It is inevitable that as you begin to create and save your maps you will want to share them with your friends, family, and other researchers with whom you may be collaborating. Or perhaps you would like to include them in a family history book, chart, blog or family website, slideshow, or video. There are endless possibilities of how to incorporate Google Earth maps into your family history storytelling! Thankfully, JPEG images can be saved directly from Google Earth for just such applications. Let's grab an image of Grandma's house in Street View.

How to Capture and Save an Image of the Map:

1. Fly to the desired location.
2. Click and drag the Street View icon over the location until the blue lines appear.
3. Drop the Street View icon directly on to the line in front of the desired location.
4. Using the navigation tools, or simply by clicking and dragging the screen, position the view as desired.
5. Click the Hide Sidebar button in the 3D Viewer Toolbar so that you will have the map image only.
6. In the Toolbar, click the Image button. (*Image right*)

7. A Save As window will pop up. Navigate to the place on your hard drive where you want to save the image.
8. Type a name in the File Name field.
9. Click OK.
10. View your image by locating it on your hard drive and double clicking on it.

(Image below: JPEG image taken from Street View of my Grandma's house today)

www.GenealogyGems.com

Because this is a JPEG image file you can use it anywhere you would normally include a JPEG file (i.e. websites, PowerPoint presentations, blogs, etc.) If you want to edit the image, you can always open it in any photo-editing program.

> **QUICK TIP:** Try Google's free Picasa photo-editing program at http://picasa.google.com/

Copying Images

Sometimes you will only need a copy of an image to quickly paste into another program, such as a PowerPoint presentation. In that type of situation you don't necessarily need to save it to your hard drive, which takes up storage space. Simply copying and pasting will do the trick.

How to Copy an Image from Google Earth:
1. From the Google Earth menu click Edit.
2. Click Copy Image which will copy the image to your computer's clipboard temporarily.
3. Open the program that you want to add the image to such as Microsoft Word.
4. Paste the image by pressing Control + V on your keyboard.

You can use this technique for any program on your computer that allows the Copy and Paste function.

Emailing Files

Sharing images via email has become second nature for most of us. And thankfully, since the last edition of this book, Google Earth's emailing featuring has improved dramatically. Simply click the Email icon in the toolbar. (*Image right*)

There are three options for what can be sent by email from Google Earth: (*Image next page*)

- Screenshot (JPEG) image of the current view of the map.
- A KML file of the current view.
- A Placemark or Folder KMZ file. In fact, any type of content (Map overlays, etc.) can be emailed with this option.

Be aware that your email recipient must have Google Earth installed on their computer (or the app on their mobile device) in order to view the 2nd and 3rd options. I have a little template I copy and paste into emails that are going to someone who I suspect may not use Google Earth. Feel free to use this in your emails:

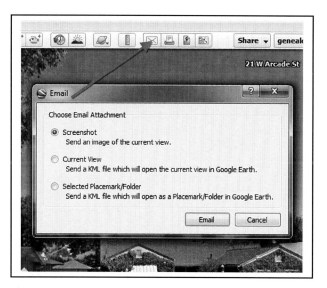

The attached file opens up in the free Google Earth program. If you don't already have it installed on your computer, you can download it for free at http://www.google.com/earth.

Email alternatives:
1. Right-click on the placemark in the Places panel, and select Email from the pop up menu.
2. From the menu click File > Email.

Printing

Good news! Printing images from Google Earth has improved as well. The biggest improvement is that you can now print or create PDFs from Street View too.

How to Print the Current View Displayed in the 3D Viewer:
1. Position the view you want (i.e. fly to the location, or double click an item in your Places panel.)
2. Click the Print button in the toolbar.
3. In the pop up box, click to select Screenshot of the Current View.
4. Click the Print button.
5. The Print dialog box will open allowing you to select your printer as the output source. If you would rather create a PDF, select a PDF printer.
6. Click the Print button.

How to Print Items in the Places Panel:
1. Click on the desired item in the Places panel.
   (Note: If your item title is hyperlinked to a website, click in the white space next to the title to select it. Clicking the title of the item will simply open the linked website.)
2. Click the Print button.
3. In the pop up box, click Selected Placemark in My Places.
   (Note: If you have selected a folder full of items, the option will say Selected Folder in My Places.)
4. The Print dialog box will open, allowing you to select your printer as the output source. If you would rather create a PDF, select a PDF printer.
5. Click the Print button.

6. The final result will print out in a columned report-type format. (*Image right*)

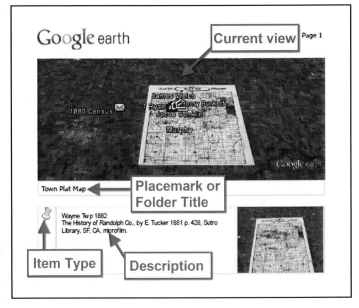

The Print feature can be accessed three ways:
- The Print button on the toolbar.
- In the menu under File > Print.
- Control + P on your keyboard.

Now that you are familiar with the methods for saving and sharing your image files you are ready to move into the next chapter where we really start to unleash the genealogical power of Google Earth. There will be many things to be shared with family and researchers alike!

Quick Tip: Font Sizing
If you find the small lettering of the labels on Google Earth a challenge to read, here's a quick solution:
1. From the menu click Tools.
2. Click Options.
3. Select the 3D View Tab.
4. In the Labels/Icon Size box select Large.
5. Click OK.

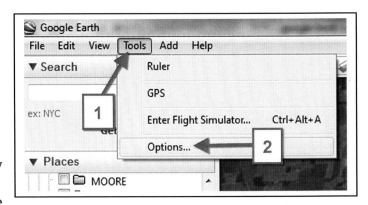

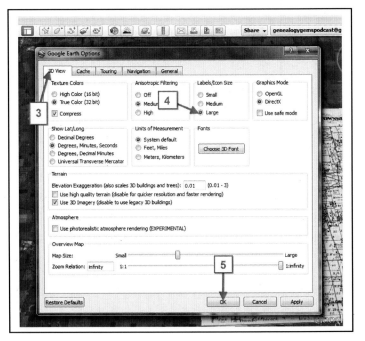

CHAPTER 18
Google Earth: Historic Images & Maps

On the surface Google Earth appears to be a modern day virtual view of our world. As you dig deeper, you'll discover there's more to it than that. Geographic history is an important element of the program, and it's available in a couple of different forms: Historical Imagery, and Rumsey Historical Maps.

Historical Imagery

Historical Imagery was first introduced in version 5.0 of Google Earth. It allows users to go back in time and study earlier stages of a location. You can view your ancestor's neighborhoods, hometowns, and other relevant places and see how they've changed over time.

(Image Right: The Historical Imagery Button on the Toolbar)

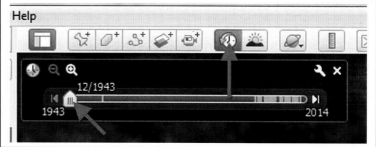

Historical Imagery includes items such as aerial and satellite photographs from government fly-overs and other sources. But one of the limitations of the Historical Imagery feature is that it can only go back as far as these images are available. If you are fortunate enough to find that Historical Imagery is available for the location you are researching, it can be very illuminating.

You'll find the Historical Imagery button (the clock icon) in the toolbar. Click it and a time slider bar will appear at the top of the map with small vertical lines on the timeline indicating how far back map images are available for your location. (*Image above*) The imagery could be older satellite imagery, or even older aerial photography. The slider will automatically be positioned at the far right side of the timeline which is the most current satellite imagery. Simply move the slider to the desired point in time. No matter what the exact point is that you release your mouse, the timeline slider will automatically move to the closest date that imagery is available.

In the case of San Francisco, we can turn the hands of time back to 1938. (*Image next page*) In the first edition of this book the oldest available imagery for this location was 1946. So as you can see, even though historical imagery is limited, imagery is being added. In fact, Google Maps added historical imagery in April of 2014 to Street View, and I predict it is only a matter of time before it makes its way to Google Earth's Street View.

To return to modern day just click the Historical Imagery icon again or move the slider back up to the current year.

How to Access Historical Imagery:
Let's look at an example of a European city damaged during WWII.

1. Type "Stuttgart, Germany" in the search box in the Search panel.
2. Click the Search button.
3. Google Earth will zoom in fairly close to the Stuttgart location on the globe.
4. Zoom out to get a broader view of the area.
5. Click the Show Historical Imagery button on the toolbar (the clock icon), which will activate the slide tool.
6. The date on the far right of the slider is very close to today's date. The date on the far left end of the slider is December 1943. Notice the marks on the slider denoting historical images available at various dates between 1943 and today.
7. Click on the slider lever and drag it all the way to the left (Dec. 1943). (*Image right*)

8. Notice that the image has changed dramatically. During WWII the city of Stuttgart was subject to over 50 air raids.
9. Zoom out to get a view of Europe. Notice the small squares of gray that appear on the map. These are areas that have historical imagery from 1943.

10. Go to the Layers panel and click the box next to Borders and Labels. This will help you identify the various countries.
11. Zoom in and out to explore the various historical images.
12. To return to modern day just unclick the clock icon or move the slider back to the current year.

Imagery from 1935 and 1945 for Warsaw in Poland is particularly compelling. The city was amongst those most badly damaged in the war and comparisons with today are striking.

See it for yourself!
Watch a brief video that demonstrates Historical Imagery.
VIDEO: *Google Earth Historical Imagery*
http://youtu.be/Nv_ScZYnsyw

Rumsey Historical Maps

http://www.davidrumsey.com

You can go even further back in time with Rumsey Historical Maps, which you will find in the Layers panel.

David Rumsey is a cartographer who has amassed a personal collection of over 150,000 historic maps. He has partnered with Google to make a few hundred of these maps available in Google Earth. Rumsey hand-picked maps to represent a cross-section of places worldwide, and time frames (1680-1930.) The maps are then "geo-referenced' to the Google Earth map, making them display in the closest way possible to the modern day map. We will be doing a bit of geo-referencing ourselves when we create our own historic map overlays.

Rumsey and his team continue to systematically digitize the collection in an effort to make them available for free at his website http://www.davidrumsey.com.

Let's try a simple exercise to see what's available. Keep in mind that all of Google Earth's features are available to use while you have an historic map overlay activated. This means that a quick way to locate the items mentioned in the exercise is still to use the Search box in the Search panel. Google Earth will fly you to that location regardless of whether a map overlay has been applied and regardless of whether or not that landmark actually appears on the historic map.

How to Activate Rumsey Historical Maps:

1. Zoom out to a wider view of the area you are interested in (ex. at least far enough out to view an entire state in the U.S., or an entire country.)
2. In the Layers panel click the small arrow next to Gallery to open it.
3. Click to check the box next to Rumsey Historical Maps. (*Image top right*)
4. Rumsey icons will appear on the map if historical maps are available for the location you are viewing. If you don't see any at first try zooming in and out.
5. Hover your mouse over the icon to reveal the date of the available map.
6. Click on the icon and a pop up window will appear with the map image and details about the map, including a link to the map on the David Rumsey website.
7. To overlay the map onto Google Earth, click on the thumbnail image of the map. (*Image bottom right*)
8. The map will spread out across the area lining up as closely as possible with the current day map. The map will resize as you zoom in and out, always maintaining proper proportions.
9. Zoom in to see all the fine details in these Rumsey maps.

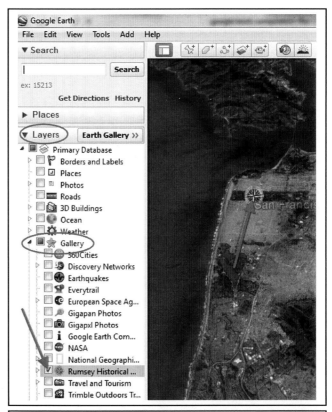

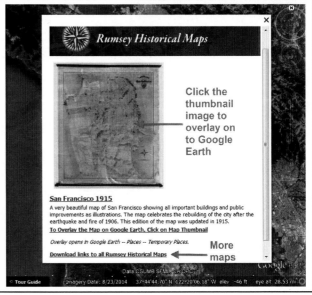

Try It for Yourself: The Streets of San Francisco

1. Type *San Francisco* in the Search box in the Search panel.
2. Zoom back out so that you can see the entire Bay Area.
3. In the Layers panel open the Gallery.
4. Click to select Rumsey Historical Maps.
5. You will see three map icons appear in the San Francisco area.
6. Hover your mouse over each of the three icons to reveal the date of each map.
7. Click on the icon for the 1915 San Francisco map.
8. A pop up window will appear with an image and details about the map.

9. To overlay the map on Google Earth, click on the map thumbnail image. (*Image below*)

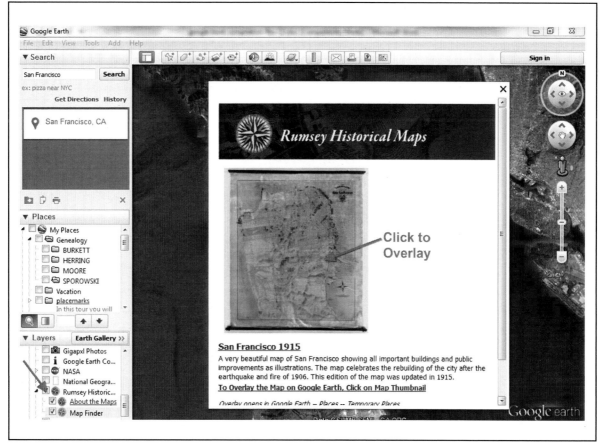

10. The map will spread across the area matching exactly (or as close as possible in the case of older maps that were somewhat inaccurate.)
11. Zoom in and out and navigate around the city. Locate the following:
    a. Balboa Park
    b. Golden Gate Park
    c. Union Square
12. In the Places panel the Adjust Opacity button can be found at the bottom of the panel just to the right of the magnifying glass button. Click it, and a slider will appear. (*Image below*) Slide the lever all the way to the left. This will adjust the

transparency back and forth so that you can make comparisons between the historic and modern day maps. Be sure that the overlay is highlighted in blue in the Places panel. This means it is selected. If it isn't, click the label "North_America..." to select it.

13. Notice that the overlay appears in the Places panel as "North_America/US..." This is a long label given to the original Rumsey map. It appears in the Temporary Places folder until you decide to delete it or save it into a permanent folder in My Places.

How to Save a Map Overlay to a Folder in My Places:
Follow these instructions to save any Rumsey map to your Places panel.
1. In the Places panel, click My Places, to select it.
2. Right click on My Places and select Add > Folder.
3. A New Folder window will pop up where you can name your folder (ex. *Maps*)
4. Enter a detailed description of its contents.
5. Click OK.
6. Scroll down the Places panel and you will see your new Maps folder.
7. Look down further to the Temporary Places folder in the Places panel. There you will find any Rumsey map that you activated in the 3D Viewer (such as the *San Francisco 1915* map from the previous exercise.)
8. Click, drag, and drop the map file into your Maps folder. The overlay can be turned on and off by clicking and unclicking the checkbox next to it.
9. Right-click the name of the map and select Rename to edit the name of the map.

While there are a number of Rumsey historic maps available in the Layers panel, wouldn't it be nice to have even more? Here's how to access all of the Rumsey maps that are included in Google Earth, and add them to your Places panel.

How to Add Additional Rumsey Maps to Your Places Panel:
1. In the Layers panel, click to select Rumsey Historical Maps.
2. Click once on one of the Rumsey icons that appears on the map.
3. In the pop up window, below the thumbnail image, click *Download links to all Rumsey Historical Maps. (Image right)*
4. In the Places panel you will see a large number of maps appear in the Temporary Places folder. (*Image next page*)
5. Close all the internal folders by clicking the little black arrows until you are left with the main folder called "Rumsey Historical Maps."
6. Right-click on the folder and click to select Save to My Places.

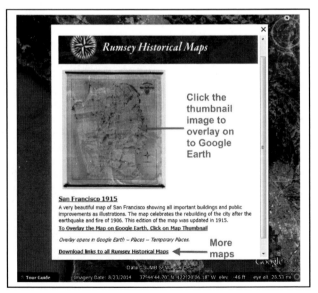

7. The folder will jump to the bottom of your My Places list. It is now part of your collection.

8. Save your work by going to File > Save > Save My Places.

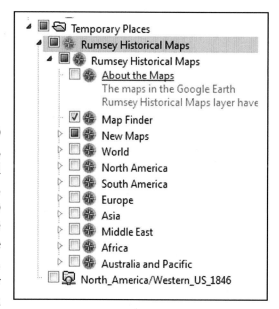

You will find hundreds of fascinating map overlays contained within these folders. However, you may notice that you are unable to click and check the box next to each main title. Instead, click the arrow to open the folder and click to select the map you want to display inside the folder. And remember, these are not large image files getting downloaded to your computer. Rather, they are maps hosted on the Rumsey website, georeferenced and ready to display via the overlays.

Also, remember that if you click the hyperlinked title, it will open the corresponding webpage on the David Rumsey website where the map originates. This can be annoying when you simply want to display the map in Google Earth. Instead, click the white space around the title on the same line to fly to that location, and click the check box to display the map.

You may find that you want to include a particular map from the collection in one of your customized family history tours which we will be creating in the final chapter. A copy of the map must be included in the map or tour folder in order for it to be included. Here's how to do it.

How to Copy a Rumsey Historical Map to another Folder:
1. Right-click on the white space around the title of the desired map.
2. Click Copy in the pop up menu. (*Image right*)
3. In My Places, right-click the folder you want to add the map to.
4. In the pop up menu, click Paste.
5. A copy of the map is now in your folder.

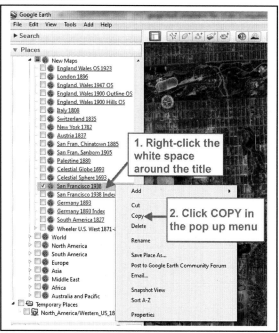

Looking for even more historical maps? Go to http://www.davidrumsey.com. At last count, there were over 44,000 high-quality, digitized maps available on the website absolutely free!

When you get to the website, scroll down until you see Map Rank Search.

This tool (*image below*) will allow you to search by place, timeframe and any text associated with the maps in the metadata. Map results will instantly appear in the column on the right.

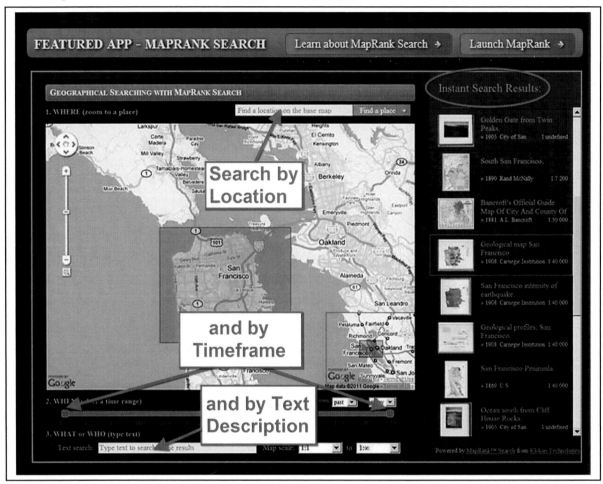

To save a copy of a map to your computer, click the Export button in the upper right corner of the map page. For the clearest detail possible, download the largest file size available.

David Rumsey's website is just one of many across the web providing access to free digitized maps. Whether you download a map, or use your own scanner to scan a paper map, you can add it to Google Earth as an overlay just like the maps that are already included in Google Earth. In the next section, I will show you how.

Creating Your Own Custom Historic Map Overlay

While Rumsey Historic Maps can be very useful in your research, unfortunately there are just a limited number available. It is possible that you may not find the ideal map for your research. Don't worry! Rumsey Historical Maps are only the beginning.

Chances are at some point in your research you've come across a Land Plat Map for an area where an ancestor lived. If you were really fortunate your ancestor's name was included on the map indicating the parcel that they owned. Wouldn't it be fantastic to add it to your Google Earth Places collection?

Here's an example (*image right*) of a plat map from a county history book now in the public domain. It shows Wayne Township in Randolph County, Indiana as it was in 1882. Owners' names and the amount of acreage they own are indicated on the map. This map would be ideal for turning into a Google Earth overlay.

How to Create Your Own Historic Map Overlay:

Step One: *Digitize the Image*
The first step to creating your own historic map overlay is to convert the map to a digital image. In this case the map could be photocopied from the book, scanned with a desktop scanner, and then saved as a picture file onto your computer's hard drive. I recommend using the highest dots per inch (dpi) your scanner can output, preferably at least 600 dpi.

If you are fortunate enough to find a map like this online you can then just save the digital image to your computer by right clicking on the image and saving it to a location of your choice on your hard drive. However, you'll want to pull it up and inspect it after you have saved it to ensure it is high enough quality to read the details. If not, consider using a screen capture program like Snagit (www.techsmith.com/snagit) to capture the highest resolution image possible.

Step Two: *Fly There*
Next, fly to the area where your map is from by entering the location name in the Search box and clicking the Search button.

Step Three: *Add Image Overlay*
There are two ways to add Image Overlays. Either method will open the New Image Overlay box and add green crosshair markers to the map.

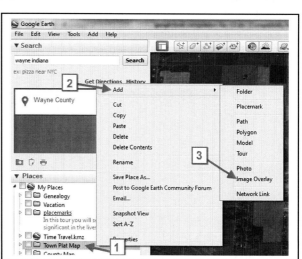

Method 1: (*Image center right*)
1. Click to select the folder in your Places panel where you want to create the overlay.
2. Go up to the toolbar and click the Image Overlay button (it looks like two pieces of paper overlaying each other.)

Method 2: (*Image bottom right*)

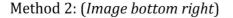

1. Go to the Places panel and right click on the folder you just created.
2. Select Add.
3. Click Image Overlay.

Step Four: *Name and Describe the Map*
You can name your historic map in the new Image Overlay box. (*Image top right*)

The description area of the box is where you would type information about the source of the map. This is much like citing sources in your genealogy database. (You may even want to use standard source citation format in this box.)

For this example I will add: "The History of Randolph County by E. Tucker published 1881. Page 428. Location: Sutro Library, San Francisco. Microfilm."

Step Five: *Attach the Map*
You can attach a map that is located on your local hard drive. If you do, however, the overlay will only work on your computer. Simply click the Browse button to locate it on your computer. However, if you want to be able to share your map and always have the overlay appear, the map image must be hosted on the cloud. An easy way to do that is to upload it to a free photo sharing website like

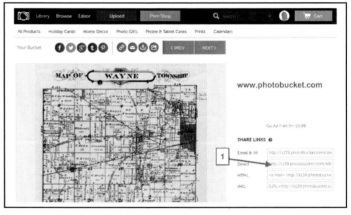

Photobucket at http://www.photobucket.com. This gives the image its own URL which you can then use in the Overlay.

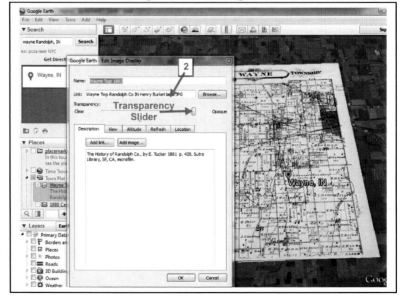

1. In Photobucket, click the Direct URL link for your uploaded image to copy it to your computer's clipboard. (*Image center right*)
2. In Google Earth, click inside the Link box and press Control + V on your keyboard to paste the image URL. (*Image bottom right*)

Note: Do not click OK or close the Overlay box. It must remain open while you adjust the map.

After a few moments the map will appear on the screen within the green placeholder lines. How long this takes depends on your internet speed.

> **QUICK TIP:** At this point you may want to hide the sidebar panel by clicking the Hide Sidebar button in the toolbar. This will give you more room to work. You can also grab and drag the Overlay box over to one side and even grab the corners of the box to make it a bit smaller, again providing more room to work.

Notice the Transparency slider tool in the Overlay box. (*Image previous page*) Slide the lever to the right and your map will become more opaque. Slide it to the left and the map becomes transparent so that you can see the current landscape beneath the historic map. This tool is critical for assisting you in sizing the map precisely to the modern day Google Earth map.

Step Six: *Matching Up Points*
Look for unique features on the historic map. What do you notice about this map of Wayne Township? Something that stands out is the very dark lines that merge together. These lines represent the railroad at that time. Look in the Wayne Township area on Google Earth to see if you can spot that railroad. Slide the transparency lever to the left to make the map transparent. Most locations have some type of distinct element that will help identify a starting point for positioning the map.

In this example we could use the point where the two railroad tracks intersect as a spot to match up with the historic map. (*Image right*) By playing with the transparency tool back and forth you can see each map until you get the points you selected lined up together.

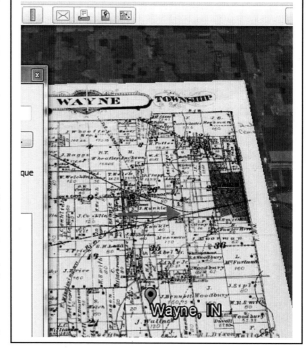

Step Seven: *Resizing the Map*
Once the maps have been lined up to match at that particular point, you'll probably notice that much of the rest of the map does not match up. That's because when you add the map it's not going to be exactly the same size as the Google Earth map. You will need to resize the overlay map until everything lines up.

You'll notice that when you hover your mouse over a green cross-hair line the hand icon turns into a pointer finger. This means that you can grab that spot and manipulate just the overlay. If you hover your mouse over the map in an area without a green line, your mouse pointer is an entire hand and that means that you'll be moving the entire map – Google Earth and your overlay together. To resize just the overlay, go to a corner and grab the green line and pull the overlay. Play with it, pulling the various corners until all the landmarks line up.

In this example I have railroad lines and a number of rivers to work with. Zoom out to give yourself enough of the Google Earth map to work with. Keep using the Transparency tool to continue checking your progress. The goal is to line up all of the landmarks throughout the map. Things may look lined up with the railroad, but the river in another corner could still be out of alignment. But in the end, if the historic map you are working with is accurate, it should line up adequately with Google Earth. Then when you use the Transparency Lever you can really see what the land of your ancestors looks like today.

Step Eight: *File Management*
Locate the map overlay you created and drag and drop it into the appropriate file folder in the Places panel if need be.

Step Nine: *Set the Transparency Level*
Before you click OK and close the map overlay box, drag the Transparency Lever all the way to the right so that your map is completely opaque. Then click OK.

Now you can see your map on Google Earth. While the overlay is activated you can adjust the transparency of the map. You will find the Transparency button at the bottom of the Places panel, right next to the search button. Click the Transparency button, and a lever will appear. (*Image right*) Slide the Transparency Lever to adjust the transparency of the map you are displaying on Google Earth. If you want to turn this overlay off so that it is invisible, uncheck the box for the map overlay in the Places panel and it will disappear. To make it visible, just click to check the box again.

Try it For Yourself:
Create Your First Custom Historic Map Overlay
Select a map from your genealogy research and create an historic map overlay in Google Earth following the nine steps above. If you don't have any old maps, locate one for one of your ancestral locations from any of the following websites that collectively hold more than 500,000 digitized maps from the U.S. and around the world:

American Memory Map Collections at the Library of Congress
http://lcweb2.loc.gov/ammem/gmdhtml/

British Library
http://www.bl.uk/onlinegallery/onlineex/mapsviews/index.html

Hargrett Rare Book & Manuscript Library
http://www.libs.uga.edu/darchive/hargrett/maps/maps.html

National Library of Australia
http://www.nla.gov.au/what-we-collect/maps suggested topics lectures

Perry-Castañeda Library Map Collection
http://www.lib.utexas.edu/maps/

Visual Collections (including the David Rumsey Collection)
http://www.davidrumsey.com/collections/cartography.html

How to Find Plat Maps Online:
1. Go to http://www.Google.com.
2. Click the Images link at the top of the page.
3. Enter keywords such as the location plus the words *plat map*. For example: *Wayne Randolph County Indiana plat map*
4. Click the Search Tools button at the top of the results list.
5. Click the various tools as needed. (*Image right*)
6. Continue to use the search skills you learned in the earlier chapters to refine your search as necessary.

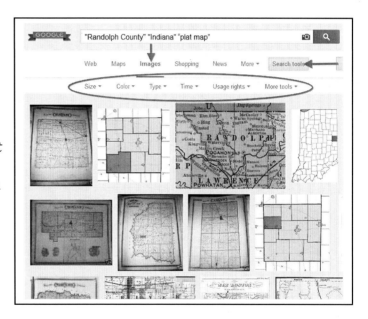

Additional Reading: Learn more about plat maps at http://en.wikipedia.org/wiki/Plat

Saving and Sharing Custom Historic Map Overlays
The maps that you create are temporarily saved to your computer hard drive. However, they are nested within the Google Earth system folders which can be a challenge to locate. They may even be stored as hidden files on your computer.

If you want to save your historic map overlays you create, it is recommended that you save them to a folder of your choosing that is easy to locate and work with.

Your maps are saved in a unique geographic format called KML. When you add an overlay or other files and save it, you are creating a zipped KMZ file folder. When opened, these files automatically launch Google Earth and display in the 3D Viewer.

How to Save Your Map Overlay to Your Computer:

1. In the Places panel, click once in the white space around the title of the file you want to save in order to select it. (*Image right*)
2. In the Google Earth menu click File > Save > Save Place As, and the Save File box will pop up.
3. Navigate to the location on your computer where you want to save your file.
4. Click Save.
5. Go to your computer's hard drive (i.e. Mac: Finder, Windows: Explorer) and locate the file you just saved.

As we discussed, it is possible to share your KMZ files. You can:

- E-mail them (right-click the file in the Places panel and select Email. The KMZ file will be automatically attached to the email.)
- Host them locally for sharing within a private Internet.
- Host them publicly on a website.

Just as web browsers display HTML files, Earth browsers such as Google Earth display KMZ files. If you're technically inclined and you decide you want to share your KMZ file online, it's just important to know that the KMZ zipped file folder must be opened and the contents extracted for them to be available on your website for use. But once you've had them uploaded properly to your website, you can share the URL of your KML files on your website and anyone who has Google Earth installed can download and view your maps.

Where Google Earth and the Census Intersect

Historic maps are powerful tools for gaining deeper insight into the lives of your ancestors. Imagine the possibilities when your genealogical records, such as the census, intersect with Google Earth and your historic map overlays!

To illustrate this, let's take a closer look at Henry Burkett's farm on the Wayne Co., Indiana plat map of 1882. (*Image next page*) You will notice that not only is Henry listed, but all of his neighbors are as well. And there is always the possibility that a neighbor or two might just be relatives!

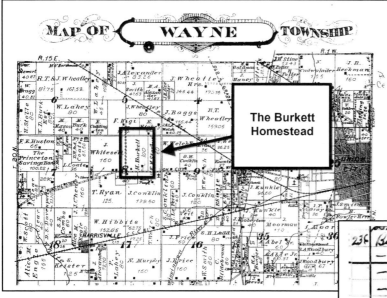

Since this example plat map is dated 1882, the closest census record to compare it to would be the 1880 U.S. Federal census.

In that enumeration, we can see that Jacob Conklin is listed just a little further down the census page. (*Image below*)

On the map, the census comes to life as we see J. Conklin with 139 and ½ acres across the road. (*Image below*) While the census can tell us the names of neighbors, it is only in combination with this historic map that the neighborhood comes into real perspective.

Keep in mind that some of the folks who look like neighbors on the census are actually living on someone else's property and therefore may not be named on the map. Perry Harrison, listed after the Conklin family, names his occupation as "Works on Farm" versus his neighbors who

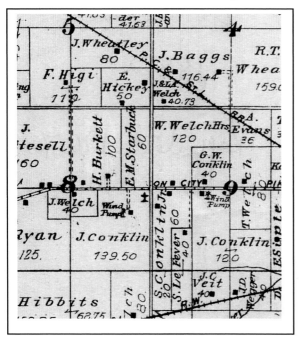

are listed as Farmer. So it is not a big surprise that Perry Harrison is not listed on the plat map because he's likely renting a place and working as hired farm labor. For the Harrison descendants, using the plat map in conjunction with the census goes a long way in helping them identify the location where Perry and his wife Martha lived even though they were not land owners.

Let's Go Visiting

Incorporating Street View can add an additional layer to the map and census that allows you to "visit" your ancestor and his census neighbors! Let's use our Wayne Township neighborhood again for this example.

Step 1:

Make the map overlay more transparent by moving the Transparency Lever (in the Places panel) to the left so that you can see Google Earth behind it. Click and drag the Street View icon over the map.

Step 2:

Blue lines will appear on the roads where Street View is available. Drop the icon on the blue line. (*Image below*)

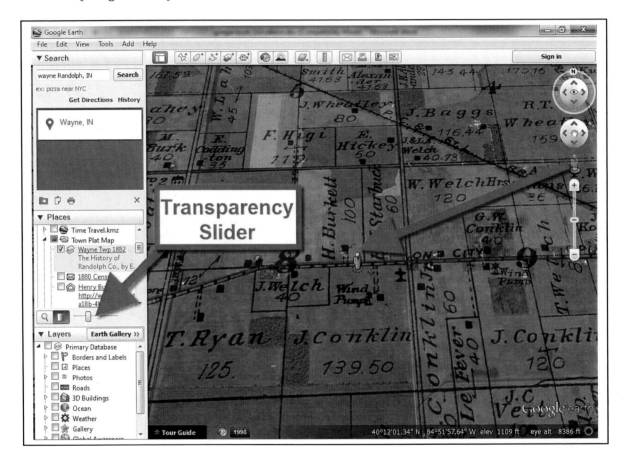

Step 3:

Zoom in closer to the farm in question. In this case, we can now see the house and barn that stand on the property today. These could very likely be the same buildings that stood there when the Burkett's lived there in 1882.

Step 4:

You will find the current address for the property today at the top of the screen.

Step 5:

Exit street view by clicking Exit Photo in the top right corner of the screen. (*Image next page*)

When it comes to getting up close and personal with your ancestors, the sky's the limit with Google Earth!

CHAPTER 19
Google Earth: Plotting Your Ancestor's Homestead

In this chapter we are going to experience how Google Earth can interact with other online websites and tools to help you explore the land your ancestors once inhabited.

Plotting an Ancestor's Homestead

In the United States, Land Patents document the transfer of land ownership from the federal government to individuals. It is very likely that at some point in your research you will come across an ancestor who received a Land Patent.

You may already be familiar with the Bureau of Land Management's General Federal Land Records website at www.glorecords.blm.gov. This is the first place you would search online for an ancestor's Land Patent Record.

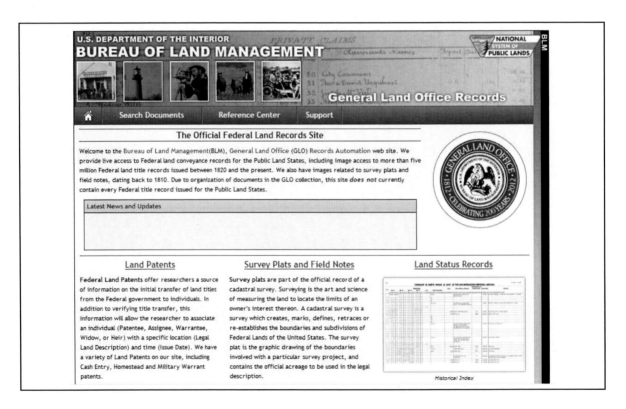

The Bureau of Land Management's General Federal Land Records website is where you can access Federal land conveyance records for the Public Land States. This website provides image access to more than three million Federal Land title records for Eastern Public Land States issued between 1820 and the present. The site is also adding images of Military Land Warrants, which were issued to individuals as a reward for their military service. However, be aware that the site still does not contain every Federal title record issued for the Public Land States. If you don't find a record you are looking for, you will need to pursue other conventional sources.

According to the Bureau of Land Management:

"The authority of many acts of Congress - sale, homesteads, disposed of the land military warrants for military service, timber culture, mining, etc. One of the primary purposes of these public land laws was to encourage people from the East to move west. In the early 1800s people could buy public land for $1.25 an acre. For a time, they could buy up to 640 acres under this law. The sale of public land under the "Cash Act" is no longer in effect.

Several Military Warrant Acts granted public land to soldiers instead of pay. These acts have been repealed.

The Homestead Act of 1862 allowed people to settle up to 160 acres of public land if they lived on it for five years and grew crops or made improvements. This land did not cost anything per acre, but the settler did pay a filing fee. This act is no longer in effect."

How to Search the BLM Website:
1. Click Search Documents from the menu.
2. You will now be on the Search Documents by Type tab. (*Image below*)

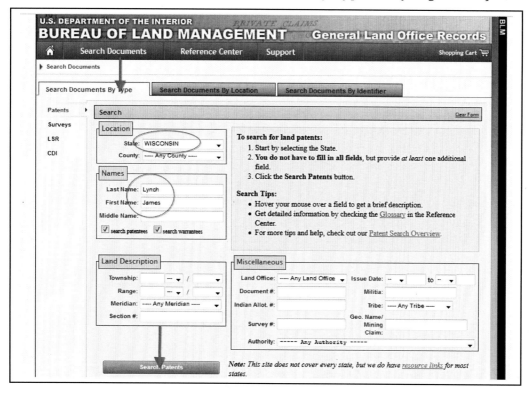

3. Select the state where you believe they owned the land.
4. Enter the Last name.
5. Enter the first name.
6. Click Search Patents.

www.GenealogyGems.com

Here is an example of search results. (*Image below*)

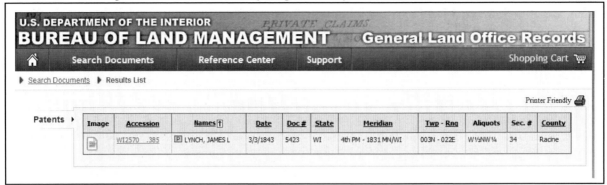

Click on the Image icon to view the original Land Patent image. (*Image below*)

QUICK TIP: Saving and Printing Land Patents
The best way to print or save a quality land patent image is to click the Document Image tab and select PDF.

Chances are if you have searched for records on this website before, you may have stopped at this point because you located the record. However, with Google Earth you can make even more use of the valuable information provided on this website.

Land Patent Details
Notice that the Accession column title is hyperlinked. Click it to be taken to the complete record. (*Image right*) Under Land Descriptions is the legal description for the property. While you can click the check box to plot the land on the map provided on the website, we're going to use the legal description to plot the land in Google Earth.

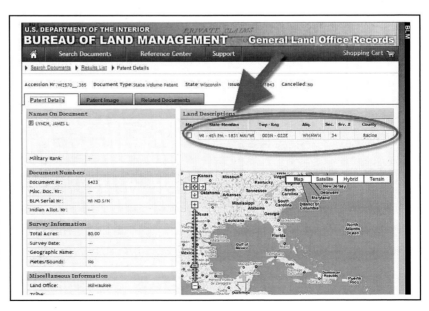

Land Descriptions						
Map	State-Meridian	Twp - Rng	Aliq.	Sec.	Srv. #	County
☐	WI - 4th PM - 1831 MN/WI	003N - 022E	W½NW¼	34		Racine

This description gives us the exact coordinates of the property. However, most of us are not prepared to use this type of data. That's where a website called EarthPoint comes in. You will find it at http://www.earthpoint.us.

The site is free, although some of the features area available only with a paid subscription. Thankfully, the tool for plotting your ancestor's land patent is free.

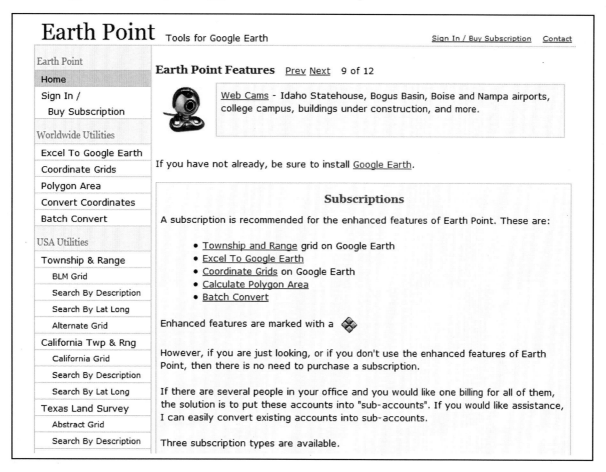

How to Plot an Ancestor's Land Patent:

1. Go to www.glorecords.blm.gov.
2. Pull up the Land Patent Details you want to plot in a web browser window.
3. In a second browser window go to www.earthpoint.us.
4. Click on the Township and Range link in the menu column.
5. Scroll down and click the link that says Convert Township, Range, and Section to Latitude and Longitude.

6. On the next page you will be entering the legal land description information. Be sure to enter the information in the order it is requested on the Earthpoint page. Each drop down menu is dictated by your previous answer. From the drop down menu, select the state.
7. Using the data from the Land Patent Details, select the Principal Meridian.
8. Select the Township.
9. Select the Range.
10. Select the Section.

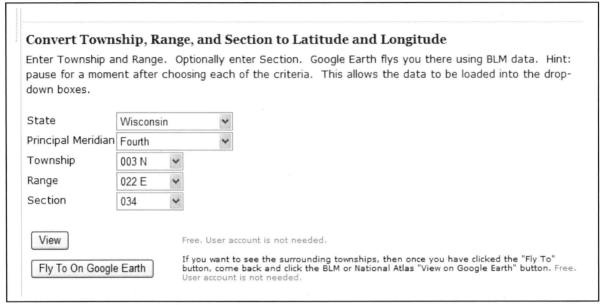

11. Click the Fly to On Google Earth button.
12. This will generate a KMZ file which will automatically open in Google Earth.
13. The KMZ file is now located in your Temporary Places folder in the Places panel.
14. Drag and drop the file into the desired folder of your Places panel. Then save your work in the menu by clicking File > Save > Save My Places.

(Image right: Earthpoint has plotted the land from the Legal Description in Google Earth)

The Township is outlined in orange, and the Section is outlined in purple. We are now looking at the exact piece of property that was described on the original land patent record! Notice that in the smaller purple square, there is a purple ball. This marks the exact center of that section. Click the ball and a dialog box providing a complete

description of the property will pop up. (*Image Right*)

How to Virtually Visit and Mark the "Old Homestead":

1. Search for a land patent.
2. View the original record.
3. View the Land Patent Details for that record.
4. Plot the Land Patent using Earthpoint in conjunction with Google Earth.
5. Zoom back out so that you can see the entire purple square outlining the section.
6. Go back to the BLM website and pull up the original land patent by clicking the index card button next to the patentee's name.

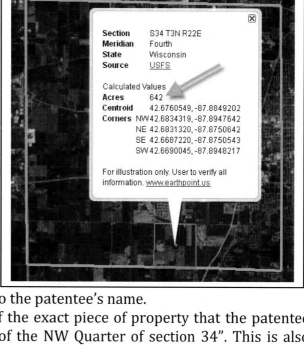

7. Find the handwritten description of the exact piece of property that the patentee received. Example: "The West half of the NW Quarter of section 34". This is also listed in the legal description under Aliquots.
8. Note how many acres were received. Example: "Containing 80 acres."
9. Go to http://www.genealogygems.tv/Pages/Store/VolII_Bonus_Content.htm and download the free acreage image that suits the property, or create your own in a graphics program.
10. Go back to Google Earth.
11. The Section is outlined in purple. Click the ball in the center and find out the total acreage of the section.
12. Locate the property according to the land patent description.
13. To delineate the acreage you have two options:
    - Upload the image you need to a photo sharing website and copy the URL. Click Add Image Overlay in the toolbar, and paste the URL. Resize the image overlay to fit. Fill in the Title and Description and click OK. (*Image right*)
    - Click the Add Polygon button on the toolbar. Click in the upper left corner of the acreage, and then click the upper right corner, and

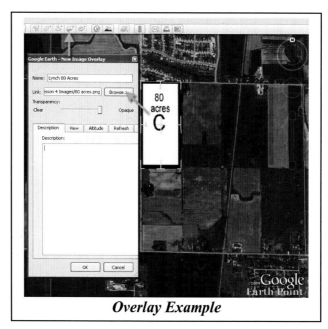

Overlay Example

so on, until the property is outlined. Click the Style, Color tab and select yellow, and make the Width of the line 2.5. Fill in the Title and Description, and click OK. (*Image below*)

Polygon Example

14. Notice that the overlay or polygon appears in the Places panel. Move the overlay or path into the appropriate folder.
15. Activate Street View.
16. Zoom in on the buildings on the property and investigate them with Street View. Which one do you think is most likely to have been the site of the original home? What is the nearby address of that location?
17. When finished, click the Exit Street View button.

Get to Know the Community

Just as we got to know the neighbors of Henry Burkett from the census and the plat map, it can be very revealing to visit the neighboring community of rural areas where our ancestors owned property. What's it like today? Are there examples of architecture still standing from that era? To find out, zoom out a bit farther and look for a nearby town, then zoom in with Street View to see what it's like.

QUICK TIP: Spotting Older Neighborhoods
A quick way to spot the older neighborhoods in a nearby town that may have examples of the older architecture is to look at the street layouts. Newer neighborhoods often have curves and cul-de-sacs. Older neighborhoods tend to be laid out in a grid pattern with few dead-end streets.

So there you have it. You have another way to look more in-depth at the land your ancestors settled. Now you don't have to wait for specials on airfares. You can visit your ancestor's homesteads yourself with Google Earth.

CHAPTER 20
Google Earth: Adding Family History Content

As you discover exciting new ways to view your family history, at some point you will want to share your findings with others: your family, other researchers, or the world at large! The good news is that with Google Earth you can, and in some very intriguing and creative ways.

In the previous chapters we explored how the census can intersect with Google Earth. But the census is just one genealogical document associated with locations. Consider virtually visiting:

- the church where your ancestors. worshipped (church records).
- the cemetery where they are buried (burial records).
- the photographer's studio where they got their portrait taken (old photos).
- the businesses where they worked (social security records).
- the distant locations where they fought in wars (military records).
- the schools they attended (educational records).

And the list goes on.

In this chapter we will incorporate your virtual visits into your custom maps with paths and polygons. We will also incorporate your genealogical documents, images, audio and video into placemarks.

Genealogical Images in Placemarks

Chances are you not only have copies of documents in the categories listed above, but also old family photos depicting some of those locations. Any type of digital image can be incorporated into a placemark. Then you will be able to simply click the placemark to view the linked images. You can incorporate as many placemarks as you would like!

How to Add an Image to a Placemark:
1. Upload the image to the internet.
   a. Your own website.
   b. A free, commercial website such as http://www.Photobucket.com.
2. In Google Earth fly to the location where you want to place an image.
3. Click the Placemark button in the toolbar.

4. Click and drag the placemark to the exact location on the map.
5. Type a name for the placemark in the New Placemark box.
6. Click the Add Image button.
7. Any website address where your image resides can be copy and pasted into the Add Image field.
8. Click the OK button next to the pasted address.
9. In the Description box, type any desired descriptive text.
10. Click the Style / Color tab if you would like to customize the placemark text in the 3D Viewer.
    a. Under the Label tab, click the color square and select the desired color of the placemark label.
    b. Adjust the number next to Scale to make the label larger or smaller.
11. To customize the placemark icon, click the icon found to the right of the placemark name at the top of the window. (*Image below*)

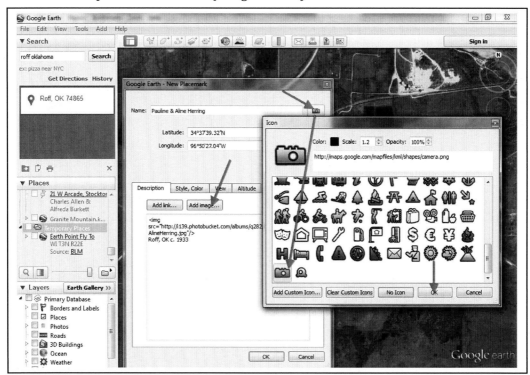

12. In the Icon window, select the desired icon. I recommend the camera icon to represent that this placemark contains a photograph.
13. Click OK to close the Icon window.
14. Click OK to finish and close the Placemark window.

Now when you click on the placemark, the photo appears in the Placemark dialog box.

You may decide after adding some placemarks that you would like to make some adjustments to them. Here's how:

How to Rename a Placemark:

1. Go to the Places panel.
2. Right-click the placemark name.
3. Select Rename.
4. Type in a new name.
5. Click OK.

How to Revise a Placemark:
1. Go to the Places panel.
2. Right-click the placemark name.
3. Select Properties.
4. Edit the Placemark window.
5. Click OK to finish.

Adding Videos to Google Earth Maps

As with images, videos can also be incorporated into your maps in Google Earth. Whether you want to include a simple home movie or an elaborate documentary-style commentary, you can do so with placemarks. Don't worry if you don't know how or don't want to create your own video. There are thousands of free videos available on websites such as YouTube that can tremendously enhance your maps, and expand on your family history.

How to Add Your Own Video to a Placemark:
1. Upload the video to a free video hosting website such as http://www.YouTube.com.
2. Click Share > Embed under the video. (*Image right*)
3. Click to highlight the code that appears in the field below. Press Control + C on your computer keyboard to copy the code to your computer's clipboard.
4. In Google Earth fly to the location where you want to place the video.
5. Click the Placemark button in the toolbar.
6. Click and drag the placemark to the desired location.

7. Type a name for the placemark in the New Placemark box.
8. Paste (Control + V) the video embed code into the Description area of the New Placemark box.
9. Under the code you can type text to accompany your video if you wish.
10. Click the Style / Color tab if you would like to change the color of the placemark. Under Label click the color square and select a color.

11. To change the placemark icon image, click the placemark icon to the right of the placemark name at the top of the window.
12. Select the movie projector or TV set icon to represent video, and click OK.
13. Click OK to finish and close the Placemark window.

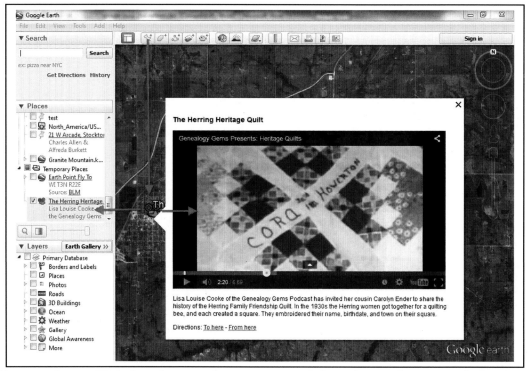

(Image above: Click the placemark icon to reveal the video in the popup dialog box. You must be connected to the internet in order to play the video.)

Troubleshooting:

If you click the icon on your map and get a white box instead of a video in the box, chances are the URL address is incomplete. This quirk has shown up recently in YouTube, and hopefully will be solved in future. For now, if you run in to this problem, there is an easy fix.

How to Fix a Missing Placemark Video:

1. Right click on the placemark.
2. Click Properties.
3. In the Edit Placemark dialog box locate the video URL in the Description area.
4. Chances are the beginning of the URL is incomplete (*Image right*). In the example on the right, the ***http:*** is missing.
5. Place your cursor at the front of the URL (immediately after ***src="***) and type in the missing letters ***http:***.
6. Click OK to close the dialog

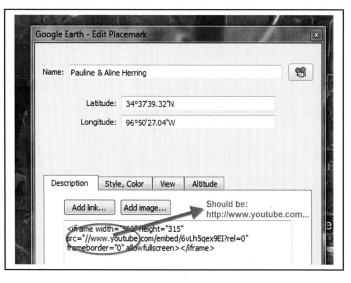

www.GenealogyGems.com

box.

7. Click the placemark and the video should appear.

As promised, you don't have to create your own video in order to enhance your Google Earth maps with video. Use the skills you developed in the YouTube chapter to locate compelling videos for your maps.

How to Add an Existing YouTube Video to a Google Earth Map:
Follow along with me as I add a video about a town where my husband's ancestors once lived to my Google Earth map:

1. In Google Earth fly to the historic seaside town of Margate, Kent, England.
2. Open your internet browser and go to http://www.youtube.com.
3. In the search box type *Margate History* and click the Search button.
4. Click on the video *Margate Sea Front 1890 – 1903*. This video is a compelling presentation of historic images set to music. (If you do not locate this video, feel free to select another from the results list.)
5. Beneath the video, click Share.
6. Click Embed.
7. Underneath the embed code, click More. Options for your video will appear such as size, and video player style. Make your desired selections. Keep in mind if the video is very large in Google Earth, it will require scrolling from side to side. I recommend the smallest size video player.
8. Notice that in the embed code the "http:' is missing from the URL address in the code. (*Image below*) Now is a good time to fix this! Type ***http:*** between the quotation mark and the two slashes just before *www*.

9. Copy the corrected embed code. (Note: The code changes based on your player selections.)
10. Go back to your Margate map in Google Earth.
11. Click the Placemark button in the toolbar.
12. Click and drag the placemark to the center of Margate if needed.
13. Type "Margate 1890 – 1930" as the name for the Placemark in the New Placemark box.
14. Paste the video embed code into the Description area of the New Placemark box.
15. Press the Enter key on your keyboard to go to the next line and type the text "Watch the video tour of Margate, Kent 1890 to 1930."
16. Click the Style / Color tab.
17. Click the color square and a blue color.

18. Click the icon to the right of the Placemark name at the top of the window.
19. Select the movie projector icon to represent video, and then click OK.
20. Click OK to finish and close the Placemark window.
21. In the Places panel, click and drag the placemark into the folder of your choice.
22. Click on the Placemark on your map to open the dialog box.
23. Click and watch the video!

QUICK TIP: Color Coding
Consider making all photograph placemarks one color, and all video placemarks another color. Or for a map with multiple families represented, consider designating a color for each family. A consistent color-coding scheme makes it quick and easy for viewers to find what they are looking for on your Google Earth map, particularly if you have included a large amount of content.

Adding Audio to Google Earth

While you may not have any home movies on video, you may have an audio recording that you would like to include. Perhaps you have an interview with a relative, or a favorite song. An easy way to incorporate audio is actually to create a video. All it takes is a free video editing software program. Here are two (one for PC, and one for Mac), but any video editing software will do:

PC: Windows Movie Maker
http://windows.microsoft.com/en-US/Windows-Live/movie-maker

Mac: iMovie
http://www.apple.com/mac/imovie/

The idea here is that you will create a very simple video, perhaps featuring just one image, with the desired audio playing in the background. (You will need to import the mp3 audio file into the video editor.) Publish it as a standard video file such as .WMV or .MP4. Then upload it to YouTube, and you can then copy the embed code and paste it into a placemark using the same method we used for video. The YouTube video player in a sense becomes your audio player. You can jazz it up by creating a slide show of multiple images, or simply include a single title slide that provides the source citation for the audio.

QUICK TIP: Make it Smaller
You may want the video player for your special audio to be smaller, since watching it is not the priority, but rather listening to it is. A much smaller player, and therefore dialog box, will allow the user to continue to be able to explore the map while listening. To achieve this, you just need to do a little

bit of editing of the embed code. While on the YouTube video page (before you copy the embed code) look for the numbers that represent the height

and the width of the video. These are generated automatically by YouTube, but you can change them. (*Image above*)

Try changing them each to 100. (*Image below*) Remember to add the "http:" to the URL while you're at it! Then copy and paste as usual.

Do you want to change the size of a video you have already included in your map? No problem! Simply re-open the placemark (right-click > Properties) and do this editing of the code right in the placemark.

Bring Focus to an Area with a Polygon

Since our goal is often to share our maps with others, it can be very helpful to provide indicators for your user as to the area you want them to focus. This can be done by outlining. An outline or border can be created with the Polygon tool found in the toolbar.

How to Outline an Area of Focus:
1. Fly back to Margate, England, or to any area pertinent to your family history that you wish to focus on.
2. Click the Polygon tool in the toolbar. A New Polygon dialog box will appear. Your cursor will now be a square.
3. Click in the upper left corner of the area on the map you want to border.
4. Click the upper right corner.
5. Click the lower left corner completing a rectangle border.
6. Hover your mouse over a corner and the mouse pointer, which is currently a square polygon tool, becomes a hand tool allowing you to click on the corners and drag them to adjust the size and shape of your polygon.
7. In the New Polygon box name your polygon *Family History Focus Area*. (*Image below*)

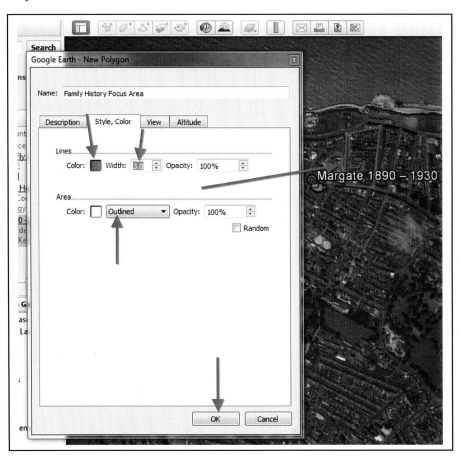

8. Click the Style / Color tab.
9. Under the Area section click the drop down box and select Outline.
10. Under the Lines section select the color you want the border to be.
11. Increase the Width of the border to 3.0.
12. Click OK to finish.

Indicate Migration with Paths

You can draw free-form paths on your map to represent the movements of your ancestors. Paths share all of the features of placemarks including name, description, style view, and location.

How to Add a Path:

1. Mark the locations you want to use to create your path with placemarks. This will help you easily find each location as you create the path.
2. Zoom in to your map as close as you can while still being able to see all of the locations. If this isn't possible, zoom to see at least the first two locations.
3. Click the Path button on the toolbar. (*Image right*)
4. The New Path box will appear, and the cursor will change to a square drawing tool.

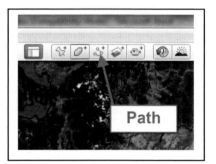

5. Enter the name and description of the path.
6. Click the Style tab.
7. Click the color box to pick the color of the path.
8. Select the desired width of the path line from the Width drop down menu.
9. Click on the locations in the order of the life events (birth to death, or town of origin to Ellis Island to their new home in America). If you need to turn the globe in order to get to the next location, click OK to close the path window. Then re-adjust your view of the map so you can see the last location and then next location. Right-click on the path and select Properties to reopen it, and then click on the next location to continue the path.
10. When complete, click OK on the New Path box.
11. Go back and delete the original placemarks if desired.

Once you have created a path, you can even play it as its own tour. Simply click on the path in the Places panel to select it. A Play Tour button will appear in the bottom of the Places panel. (It will have the path icon on it.) Click the button and the path tour will begin to play and move from location to location. Even better, include the path as part of a greater family history tour that pulls together all of the exciting content you've assembled. And that is our next chapter!

CHAPTER 21
Google Earth: Family History Tours

Geographic locations are a critical part of genealogical research. Maps can reveal patterns, terrain obstacles, and other key factors that can help you better understand your ancestors' lives. Maps can also help reveal the next logical places to look for more clues. By pulling together all of the elements you've been working with so far, you can create what I like to call a *Family History Tour. Tours* can be shared with your family, and used as a powerful reference tool in your research. You can customize and create your own maps in the Places panel and save them to your computer. You can even record a tour of your map for sharing.

Let's talk about the components of a *Family History Tour.* Some of the things you can include are:
- Custom placemarks representing life events at various locations (births, school, marriage, residences, ports of immigration, deaths, etc.)
- Photos
- Additional text and stories
- Paths representing movements
- Overlays of historic maps and images

A *Family History Tour* tells a story. Here are some ideas for stories you may want to tell through a tour:
- Migration
- Catastrophic events
- Ancestors' work history
- 2 families that join through marriage
- History of a village

Start by creating an outline of what your tour will cover. An outline helps you organize the events, and determine the size. Remember, sometimes less is more. If you overwhelm your viewer with information they will likely tune it all out, particularly the non-genealogists in your life! If your goal is to tell a compelling story, strive for a beginning, middle and end, with only the juiciest parts included. If the purpose of the tour is a research tool, then by all means add everything including the kitchen sink.

The beauty of a Google Earth Family History tour is that you can include as much content as you want, but only activate the content you want to show by clicking the check boxes. And a tour can actually be more like a chapter of the story. In other words you can break the story up in to multiple folders, and nest them all within one larger folder, or simply have them stand alone. Again, depending on the story you want to tell, you click to activate the appropriate content.

Investing time up front in planning your tours will make the production process much easier, and you will be more likely to have an end product that pleases you.

So, let's begin by creating a folder for your tour.

How to Create a Family History Tour Folder:
1. In the Places panel, right click on My Places.
2. Click to select Add > Folder.
3. Name the folder (e.g. *John Smith Life Tour*).
4. Type additional details describing the tour into the description box if desired.
5. Click OK.

The new folder now resides in your Places panel. The folder's checkbox will be checked, which means you are currently working on and viewing the contents of this folder. Click the folder once to select it. Now, each item you add point will be saved to this folder.

Adding a Family History Tour Guide Placemark
I recommend creating a custom placemark to alert your viewer where to begin.

How to Create a Tour Placemark:
1. Fly to the general area where your recorded tour will begin.
2. Click the Add Placemark button in the toolbar.
3. Move the placemark on the screen to a location where it can be easily found but doesn't interfere with other content.
4. In the Add Placemark box type a title such as *Start Tour Here*.
5. In the Description area you have the opportunity to add text that sets the stage for your tour.
6. Click the icon in the upper corner of the Placemark window.
7. Select the image you want to represent your tour.
8. At the top of the Icon window increase the Scale to 2.0 so that the Tour Guide icon will stand out, and click OK.
9. Click OK to close the Placemark box.
10. Now you can click on the Tour Guide icon on your map to introduce your viewer to your tour. (*Image right*)

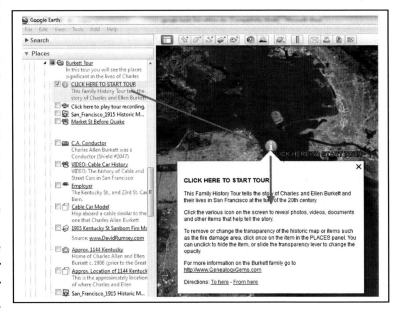

While there is an assortment of placemark icons to choose from in step 7 in the above instructions, there may be times when none of the choices will do. That's when you will want to add your own custom placemark icon.

www.GenealogyGems.com

How to Add Your Own Custom Placemark Icon:

1. Go to http://www.google.com to conduct an image search for an icon graphic. For my map, I want to add a cable car icon to represent the location where my Great Grandfather worked on the cable cars in San Francisco at the turn of the 20th century. At Google.com I would search on *"cable car" "icon"* and then click Images. (*Image top right*)

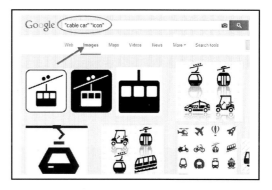

2. If you wish to further refine your results, click the Search Tools button.

3. Click the image you want.

4. Click the Visit Page button to go to the website where the image is hosted to determine copyright usage.

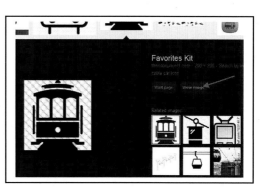

5. If copyright use permits, go back to the result, and click the View Image button. (*Image center right*)

6. Right-click on the image, and select Save Image As.

7. Save the image to the desired location on your computer.

8. Create a new placemark, or right click an existing one and select Properties to open the placemark window.

9. Click the placemark icon in the upper right corner of the window.

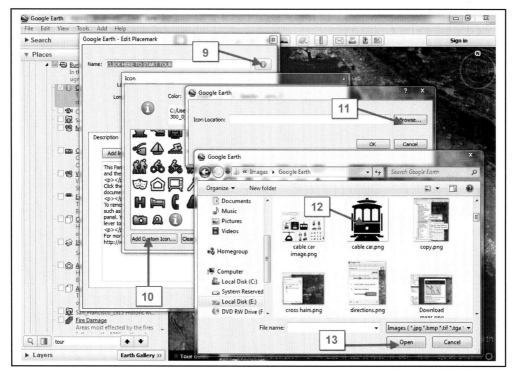

10. In the Icon window, click the Add Custom Icon button.

11. Click the Browse button and navigate your way to the icon image you just saved to your computer.

12. Click the icon to select it.
13. Click Open.
14. Click the OK buttons to close each of the windows. The icon now appears on the map and in the tour folder in My Places. (*Image below*) Note: In order to change the color of the image, you will need to recolor it in a photo editor program before adding it as an icon.

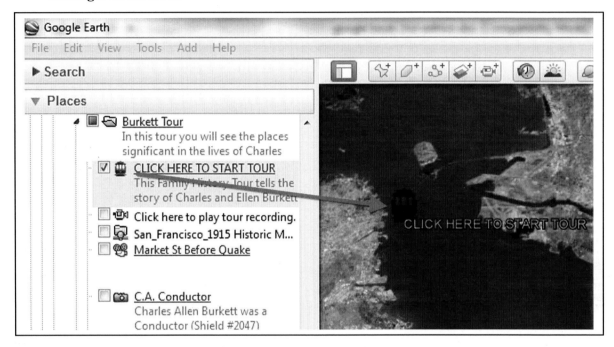

Now it's time to start adding content.

How to Add "Life Event" Icons to the Map:

1. Fly to the location where the life event occurred.
2. Click the Placemark icon on the toolbar.
3. A New Placemark window will appear.
4. Type in a name for the event in the Name field.
5. Enter a detailed description or story in the Description section.
6. Click the icon button in the top right corner of the box to reveal an assortment of icons. (*Image right*)
7. Click the icon that best represents the life event, or add an icon to the Custom Icon Gallery, or add your own as we discussed previously.
8. Adjust the color, scale, and opacity of the icon at the top of the box if desired.

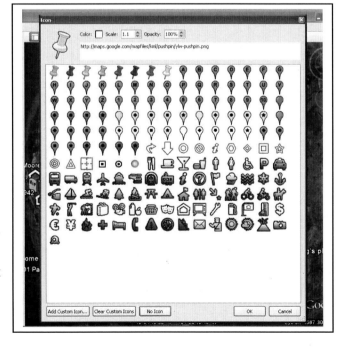

9. Click OK.

The Life Event placemark now appears in the tour folder in your Places panel.

Continue to add additional placemarks for life events such as photos, scanned historical documents, video and audio. There may be occasions when there is a website that would be the perfect companion to a placemark. Since websites are already hosted on the internet, they are super easy to add.

How to Add a Website Link to a Placemark:
1. In a web browser, go to the webpage you want to add.
2. Copy the webpage's URL.
3. Create a new placemark or open an existing placemark.
4. In the Edit Placemark window, click the Add Link button. (*Image top right*)
5. Paste the URL into the Add Link field.
6. Click the OK button next to the field.
7. Click the OK button at the bottom of the Edit Placemark window to close it.
8. Click the placemark icon on the map.
9. In the pop up dialog box you will now see the website link. (*Image bottom right*)
10. Click the link and the website will open in the browser in Google Earth.
11. Click the Back to Google Earth button to close the browser.

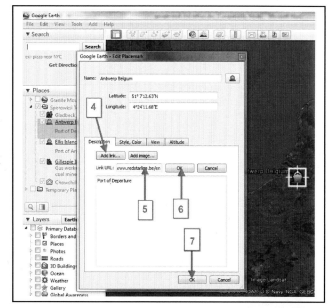

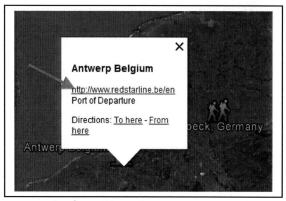

If the website doesn't open in a browser in Google Earth but instead opens in your regular web browser, you will need to change the program's settings.

How to Change Web Browser Settings in Google Earth:
1. In the main menu click Tools.
2. Click Options.
3. Click the General tab.
4. Under Display, uncheck the box for "Show web results in external browser."
5. Click the Apply button.
6. Click the OK button to close the window.

www.GenealogyGems.com

Recording a Family History Tour

Now that you have compiled all that interesting content, you can share it with your family, friends, and fellow researchers by recording your tour.

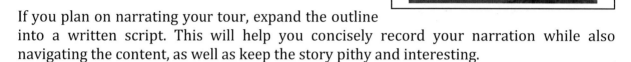

Start with the outline you already created. Sort your content in the folder to match your outline. This will make it much easier to stay on track as you navigate the map during the recording session.

If you plan on narrating your tour, expand the outline into a written script. This will help you concisely record your narration while also navigating the content, as well as keep the story pithy and interesting.

The Record a Tour button looks like a video camera and is located on the Google Earth toolbar. (*Image above right*) When clicked, a small recording panel will appear in the bottom of the 3D Viewer. (*Image right*) You have two recording options:

1. Silently record only the screen movements by clicking the red circle button.
2. Record the screen and your audio narration by clicking the microphone button.

If you have a microphone built in to your computer, it will record the audio. However, you can also record audio by plugging an external microphone into your computer.

How to Record a Family History Tour:
1. Click to select your tour folder in the Places panel.
2. Fly to the location where you want to begin your tour.
3. Click the Record a Tour button on the toolbar.
4. A small recording panel will appear in the bottom of the 3D viewer.
5. Press the red Record or Microphone button depending on whether or not you wish to record audio.
6. Following your outline, navigate the map as you wish for it to be seen in the recording, highlighting placemarks and other noteworthy content. Start with all of the content boxes unchecked except for the Tour Guide placemark. This will keep your map clean and simple when you begin. Click the white space around the title of the first item in the Places panel to fly to that location. Then click the check box for the location when you are ready to reveal it. With a little practice, you can navigate smoothly and with purpose. Continue navigating through the items, checking and unchecking boxes to reveal content as desired.
7. When finished, pause a few seconds and then click the red button again to stop.
8. The recorded tour will automatically begin to play back in the player bar at the bottom of the screen.

9. Click the Save button on the player and a New Tour window will open. (*Image right*)

10. Type a name for the tour. I like to name mine something like "Click here to play tour" so that the folks I send the KMZ file to will find it easy to use.

11. Type a description of what the tour will cover.

12. Click OK.

13. From the menu click File > Save > Save My Places to save your work.

QUICK TIP: Recording

Let the recorder run a few extra seconds after you have finished before you stop the recording. This will ensure that your recording is not cut short prematurely as Google Earth can sometimes shave a few seconds off the recording.

As a tour plays, the viewer can "look around" by clicking and dragging the map. This will temporarily pause the tour. When the play button is clicked again, the tour resumes where it left off.

QUICK TIP: Highlighting Video Content in a Tour

If you click on a placemark that contains a video during the recording of your tour, don't attempt to play it. It will not appear to play in the recorded tour. Instead, it is better to demonstrate to your viewer that the video is available by simply clicking the placemark to reveal that it contains a video. The viewer can play the video right from the tour view if they wish. You could even add text to the description such as "click the video play button to play the video, and then click the tour play button to resume the tour." Keep in mind that you are not screen capturing. Rather, you are recording a geographic tour which is a KML/KMZ file, not a true standard video such as an MP4.

See It In Action!
VIDEO: *Google Earth Tour Creation Video*
http://youtu.be/nuJwarqTLQA

Saving and Sharing Tours

Now it's time to zip up and save your tour folder into a neat little package that can be shared.

How to Save Your Family History Tour:
1. In the Places panel, right-click the tour folder and select Save Place As.
2. In the pop up window name the file as desired.

3. Save it to the desired location on your computer, such as your desktop. Be sure to leave the file type as KMZ.
4. Click OK.
5. Close Google Earth.
6. Go to the location on your computer where you saved your file.
7. Click on KMZ file you just created. This will automatically re-launch Google Earth, and display all of the saved tour content.
8. Click on the various content icons to test them.

QUICK TIP: What You See is What You Get
Keep in mind that any layers (in the Layers panel) that you had activated at the time you created and saved your file will also appear in the final KMZ file. For instance, if you have Borders and Labels activated, or 3D Buildings activated, those items are going to appear in addition to your tour content. This might clutter the map and confuse the viewer. It's best to de-activate any layers not directly pertaining to the family history tour before saving it.

Sharing Content-Rich Family History Tours
Now that your family history content is neatly packaged into a KMZ file it's ready to be sent to family, friends and fellow researchers. The easiest way to do that is to email it. Simply open your preferred email program, create a new email message, and attach the KMZ file that you saved to your desktop. When the recipient opens the file it will automatically launch in Google Earth, providing they have Google Earth installed on their computer.

QUICK TIP: Make It Easy on Recipients
Consider including a link to the Google Earth download page in your email for the folks who receive your emailed KMZ family history files. For example you could add the following to the end of your email: "To view the attached file, download Google Earth for free at http://earth.google.com". That way they can easily download the free program before launching your file.

Conclusion
Storytelling is an important piece of the genealogical puzzle. A good story is hard for even the non-genealogist to resist. Now with Google Earth you will be able to create and share compelling stories of your family history.

APPENDIX
Find It Quick: The "How To" Index

How to:

ABOUT THE AUTHOR

Lisa Louise Cooke is the owner of *Genealogy Gems*, a genealogy and family history multi-media company. She is producer and host of the *Genealogy Gems Podcast*, the popular online genealogy audio show available at www.GenealogyGems.com, in iTunes, and through the free *Genealogy Gems* Toolbar. Her podcasts bring genealogy news, research strategies, expert interviews and inspiration to genealogists in 75 countries around the world.

Lisa is the author of a variety of multi-media materials including the *Genealogy Gems Premium* website subscription, her book *Genealogy Gems: Ultimate Research Strategies* (paperback, digital download, and for iPad), and the DVD series *Google Earth for Genealogy.*

In addition to *Genealogy Gems*, Lisa works closely with *Family Tree Magazine* as producer and host of the *Family Tree Magazine Podcast*, a regular article author for the magazine, and curriculum developer and instructor for Family Tree University.

Lisa's offerings are not limited to online. She is a sought after international genealogy speaker, and produces live presentations of *The Genealogy Gems Podcast* at top genealogy conferences.

Whether in person or online, Lisa strives to dig through the myriad of genealogy news, questions and resources and deliver the gems that can unlock each listeners own family history treasure trove!

Genealogy Gems

GET MORE GENEALOGY GEMS
www.GenealogyGems.com

Online:

Listen to the Genealogy Gems Podcast

Genealogy Gems Premium Annual Membership
(Videos and Audio)

Family History: Genealogy Made Easy Podcast

Books:

How to Find Your Family History in Newspapers

Turn Your iPad into a Genealogy Powerhouse

Genealogy Gems: Ultimate Research Strategies

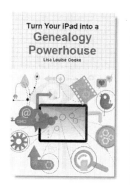

DVDS:

Google Earth for Genealogy Volume I

Google Earth for Genealogy Volume II

Quick Reference Guides:
Evernote for Windows for Genealogists

Evernote for Mac for Genealogists

Live Presentations, Seminars and Webinars:

Email your booking inquiry to genealogygemspodcast@gmail.com

Suggested Topics: http://lisalouisecooke.com/presentations/bookings/